AF538551

HUMAN RIGHTS AND PEDAGOGY

By
Sandeep Kumar
Assistant Professor
Department of Education
University of Delhi
Delhi, (India)

D P H

DISCOVERY PUBLISHING HOUSE PVT. LTD.
NEW DELHI-110 002

Published by:
Tilak Wasan

DISCOVERY PUBLISHING HOUSE PVT. LTD.
4383/4B, Ansari Road, Darya Ganj
New Delhi-110 002 (India)
Phone : +91-11-23279245, 43596064-65
Fax : +91-11-23253475
E-mail : parul.wasan@gmail.com
discoverypublishinghouse@gmail.com
web : www.discoverypublishinggroup.com

***First Edition:* 2012**

ISBN: 978-93-5056-099-0

Human Rights and Pedagogy

Printed at:
Shree Balaji Art Press
Delhi

Preface

Human Rights are always seen as an asset we all should have. We, almost all the people working and studying in the field of social science are aware of the concept of human rights. Generally, we understand human rights with reference to social and political context. At times it is also talked about in the context of the rights of different marginalized sections of society. But have we ever tried to understand it from a pedagogic perspective? There was a huge debate about including human rights in school education as a separate subject or within the curriculum or content of syllabus. But what if I say we can use it as pedagogy? This book is trying to explore the possibilities of using human rights perspective in teaching learning processes. It provides a framework to help teachers and teacher educators to develop an understanding about human rights and its implications for pedagogy. I accept that in the last couple of years many books have been published in India. None of them have talked about or made a direct reference to human rights implications for pedagogy. But this work is different from them as it specifically provides an elaborate understanding about pedagogy based on human rights perspective. It does not only deals with strategies, techniques and methods, but also extensively deals and talks about a comprehensive understanding about human rights perspective-based teaching/learning processes.

I accept this book is not intended to be the be all and end all on this field but rather a new beginning. I believe teachers and teacher educators will read and use these ways to be more humane in their teaching learning processes and will develop a feeling of concern towards their students. I also believe that they will develop their own ways to become a humane teacher, after reading this work. I am sure we all know that there is no single strategy or method which is universal so, it is better to be open minded in terms of perspective which we use and that with which students come to study.

I hope this book at least will help you to innovate so that you are capable of developing your own framework, to be a good pedagogue based on the human rights perspective.

SANDEEP KUMAR

Acknowledgements

This Resource Book would not be possible without the cooperation of the teachers who allowed me to observe their classes. I am thankful to them for their support.

I am also thankful to the experts who shared their valuable ideas to make this work possible.

I am also thankful to Chandan Shrivastav, who helped me to develop the cover page of this resource book.

Last but not the least a word of thanks is also due to the University of Delhi for providing financial support to conduct this research project.

SANDEEP KUMAR

Contents

UNIT TWO
What is the Need?

Introduction

When we starts thinking about rights and specially about Human Rights, that thinking process leads us beyond the boundaries of one nation. Because the concept of Human itself is universalized and we can not do justices with it if we think about this in a very narrow regime like within the boundaries of a nation. It is necessary to know the global perspective of human rights whether we are locating it in national context or international context. There is no place and context where we can think without Human Rights Perspective, whether we talk about society or economy or politics etc. If we go little more comprehensively we will find it in daily life of a person, where he/she is going to buy something, using public services, studying in school etc. The scope of Human Rights has been identified in all aspect of a human being or it should be said in all aspects of living beings.

This is not new what I am going to say here. It is just we have general attitude to listen, see and forget. Think for a while about people living on road side, children and old persons begging on signals, people living under flyovers, children collecting garbage, people with disability asking money for food.

I am sure you and your loving ones have not faced such a situation. But have you ever thought about all this or thought and forget after some time or you are very much keep thinking about this. Put yourself the categories you want and again think about it. You will feel an inside pain, you will not be able to eat;

you will not be able to sleep. Something will bite you from inside. But if you can sleep after seeing such situation, then I have another question for you, ARE YOU A HUMAN BEING?

By saying all this, intention is not to let you feel very low but certainly yes my intention is to make you feel uncomfortable with the existing situation. My intention is to realize you to rethink about your thinking. My intention is to make you understand that the life is a pain for some one. My intention is to aware you that every one is not so lucky to have even one time meal. My intention is to tell you that millions have no roof and clothes in 2 degree Celsius temperature. My intention is to help you to be mankind. My intention is to make you feel the feel of such marginalized people.

I hope now you can think the scope of existence of Human Rights. As it has been mentioned that Human Rights exists everywhere, so this work will try to make you understand what Human Rights Perspective exist in schools, specially in pedagogy of social sciences. Also it will provide a better understanding how to be more humanitarian in our classes or in pedagogy are to be used.

Human Rights education is an emerging concept and has assumed eminence and special significance in order to ensure success of democracy, socialism and secularism throughout the world. Human Rights Declaration proclaimed certain explanation about Human Rights—

- All human beings are born free and equal in dignity and rights.
- Everyone is entitled to this right without discrimination of race, colour, sex, language, conviction, personal opinion, property, and birth and other status.
- Every one has right to life, liberty and security etc.

But we know the reality. Above declaration is only on the papers not in reality. We can see many cases such as:-

- Working children from age 6-14 in India are 10.4 million (National Survey, 2004).
- In 2006, 13,449 cases of SC/ST exploitation were notified. (Labour and Employment Ministry, 2007).
- Pinki (15 years old) found dead after teachers punishment in 2007 (Dinkar Model School).

There are other millions of such cases which force us to think about the contribution of education to make people sensitive and concern about all these issues.

So we all know Human Rights are very important for the development of humanity, but it is a different issue all together that how we perceive Human Rights. Today, many subjects are taught as a compulsory subjects to all pupils up to secondary level. Do we bother about their contribution to the development of Human Rights understanding and applicability? Do we think how can we use Human Rights perspective in curriculum and course content development? Do we ever think, can we use Human Rights perspective in pedagogy of different subjects? Certainly we do not bother about all these questions.

So it become necessary to understand the position of Human Rights in school education, so that a healthy perspective of Human Rights can be developed and can fined out possible implication of Human Right for curriculum, course content, pedagogy, evaluation etc.

Above understanding shows that we need a powerful educational system (Mechanism) which deal to promote human rights, which also helps us to come out from theory to practicability about human rights.

Present work is trying to locate the applicability of human rights perspective in pedagogy of social science teaching. For this purpose classroom observations, discussion with teacher and interview experts have been conducted.

It should be mentioned here that there is no such book available for the teacher. Moreover the development of the book employ a collaborative approach in which teachers, school, and experts have contributed.

Above understanding highlights the need to understand the Human Rights perspective in education and pedagogy. With broad aim data was collected from classroom observation, discussion (informal) with social science teachers and interviews with experts in the field of Human Rights. Only one school was taken to observe the social science classes (class VIII, IX, X). Total 30 classes were being observed. Informal interactions were also done with the school teachers whose classes were being observed to have a better and deeper understanding about the situation. Views of three experts have also been taken for this purpose (Dr. Sanjay Dubey, Director, NHRC, Prof., Nalini Juneja, NUEPA and Dr. N. Sukumar, Delhi University).

This entire resource book will try to help you to understand the followings:

- Understanding of Human Rights.
- What Human Rights Education is all about?
- What are teachers and experts view about human rights perspective for pedagogy?
- What is the classroom situation in terms of pedagogy from human rights perspective?
- What are the common identified issues related to this teaching learning perspective?
- What are the possible solutions of these problems?
- How can we make a class human rights perspective-based class?

Therefore the aim of this work is to provide support to teachers to enhance their understanding of social science and to become more competent in the pedagogical aspects of social science with special reference to human rights.

This resource book is divided into two units and each unit has different chapters.

Unit One presents a theoretical background or a theoretical perspective about Rights and Human rights in details. It includes total three chapters—*First chapter* talks about an overview of Human Rights, *second chapter* deals with the understanding of Human Rights Education and *third chapter* includes the thematically analysis of the collected date from different sources.

Unit Two is presenting the need of the pedagogy with respect to Human Rights Perspective. It presents a full programme regarding how to include Human Right in Pedagogy. This unit includes four chapters. *Fourth chapter* is providing an understanding that only reform in pedagogy is not sufficient, so it present worksheets and resources sheet-based programme to education learners and teachers about the notion and understanding of human rights. *Chapter fifth* deals with the inclusion of human rights in pedagogy. *Chapter sixth* with continuum to this talk about the kind of environment we need for the class to make it more human rights perspective based. *Seventh chapter* includes some innovative ideas regarding human right perspective and education specially pedagogy.

UNIT ONE

Understanding Human Rights: Theory and Praxis

This unit specifically deals with an overview of Human Rights. It includes history ans concept of human rights in western context as well as Indian context it also discuss the different types and generation of human right. This unit will also help to explore the concept of Human Right Education. After this theoretical understanding, this unit also talks about what exits in praxis. It includes the analysis of classroom observation and analysis of experts' views about human rights and its inculusion in pedagogy.

1

Human Rights

An Overview

HISTORY, CONCEPT AND CONCERNS

Rights that belong to an individual as a consequence of being human. The term came into wide use after World War II, replacing the earlier phrase 'natural rights', which had been associated with the Greco-Roman concept of natural law since the end of the Middle Ages. As understood today, human rights refer to a wide variety of values and capabilities reflecting the diversity of human circumstances and history. They are conceived of as universal, applying to all human beings everywhere, and as fundamental, referring to essential or basic human needs. Human rights have been classified historically in terms of the notion of three 'generations' of human rights. The first generation of civil and political rights, associated with the Enlightenment and the English, American, and French revolutions, includes the rights to life and liberty and the rights to freedom of speech and worship. The second generation of economic, social, and cultural rights, associated with revolts against the predations of unregulated capitalism from the mid-19th century, includes the right to work and the right to an education. Finally, the third generation of solidarity rights, associated with the political and economic aspirations of developing and newly decolonized countries after World War II, includes the collective rights to political self-determination and economic development. Since the adoption of the Universal Declaration of Human Rights in 1948, many treaties and agreements for the protection of human rights have been concluded through the auspices of the United Nations, and several regional systems of human rights law have been established. In the late 20th century ad hoc international criminal tribunals were convened to prosecute serious human rights violations and other crimes in the former Yugoslavia and Rwanda. The International Criminal Court, which came into existence in 2002, is empowered to prosecute crimes against humanity, crimes of genocide, and war crimes.

The concept of human rights has evolved over time, and various countries have emphasized different aspects of human rights principles and policy. Some nations have emphasized traditional civil and political rights (both individual and collective), whereas others—particularly communist and socialist regimes—have emphasized the concept of economic and social rights. Some governments have embraced both sets of principles.

In the United States, the concept of certain individual and collective rights—in particular, civil and political rights—as 'natural' or 'unalienable' can be traced back to colonial times, reflecting the influence of John Locke and other political theorists. This concept was clearly set forth in the Declaration of Independence and was codified in the Constitution and the Bill of Rights. The United States has long regarded international human rights standards as universal. It has rejected the arguments of nations such as China, which claim that such standards can be discounted as mere 'Western' concepts and argue that human rights should be viewed through the prism of each nation's history and culture. Unlike many governments, the United States acknowledges that some human rights problems persist within its territory despite its generally good record and accepts that universal human rights standards involve study and criticism of such matters. If we try to locate the origin of the notion of human rights, we have to back to the Code of Hammurabi, 1750 B.C.E. Hammurabi was a ruler of Babylonia—one of the several rival Mesopotamian kingdoms—whose reign marked a golden age of Semitic culture. Hammurabi eventually conquered the other Mesopotamian kingdoms, and issued a law code 'to establish justice throughout Mesopotamia'.

Clay tablet records show that Hammurabi was a scrupulous, able administrator. His code—one of the earliest legal documents—influenced near eastern civilization for centuries. It consolidated earlier regulations (of the formal rival kingdoms Akkad and Sumer) on practical aspects of trade, labor, property, family, slavery, and the eye for an eye, tooth for a tooth punishment. The Code of Hammurabi survives in a stone column discovered in Iran in 1901 (now in Paris), and in clay tablet versions, probably originally posted to inform literate citizens of their rights.

Confucius—*c.* 551 - *c.* 479 B.C.E. was a philosopher who taught government and social reform. His philosophical teachings revolved around jen or benevolence, which he expressed in twin sayings: "Do not do to others what you would not like yourself" and:

"Do unto others what you wish to do unto yourself".

He believed that people should practice jen towards those below them in a social or spiritual hierarchy and that government should practice jen rather than use force. His own employment in government was troubled by disagreements with his superiors. Confucian teachings emphasizing the individual's responsibilities to the community remain influential to this day in China and other Asian countries.

English nobles and clergy rallied against King John I's abuse of power—heavy taxation to finance expensive, unsuccessful wars, and his refusal to accept papal authority, which effectively kept churches closed for years. They subjected the King to the rule of law by enacting from him a 'great charter' of liberties.

Though King John I soon violated it, the *Magna Carta* (1215) eventually came to be cited widely, in defense of many liberties. The U.S. national and state constitutions contain ideas and even phrases directly traceable to it, for example, the concept of no taxation without representation. Clause 39, which stated that "no free man shall be arrested or imprisoned...[or dispossessed] except by...lawful judgement," became known as the right of *habeas corpus*, or due process of law.

English Bill of Rights, 1689

James II, like several kings before him, thought the law inconvenient and often dispensed with it. For this his subjects overthrew him in 1688, and when Mary II and William III took the throne in 1689, Parliament passed a bill declaring that it would no longer tolerate royal interference in its affairs. The bill became part of the foundation of the English Constitution, and in the following century, most English took pride in the freedom its provisions gave them from arbitrary government.

The bill forbade royalty to suspend law without Parliament's consent, specified free elections for members of Parliament, and declared that freedom of speech in Parliament was not to be questioned, in the courts or elsewhere. The bill also prohibited taxation or maintenance of an army in peacetime without Parliament's consent, excessive bail or fines, and cruel and unusual punishment.

United States Declaration of Independence, 1776

Calling themselves the Continental Congress, representatives of Britain's 13 colonies first convened in 1774 to protest against British policies. When they convened again after the American Revolution had begun, they voted for independence from Britain and adopted the Declaration of Independence, becoming the first government of the 13 United States. The Declaration had far- reaching and lasting influence on individual rights in western civilization, inspiring rebellion against Spanish rule in South America and against monarchy in France.

Because of his literary skill, Thomas Jefferson was chosen to write the Declaration. Based largely on Locke's and Montesquieu's 'natural rights' theories, it listed the colonists' grievances against King George, accusing him of systematic tyranny; announced the colonies' separation from Great Britain; proclaimed the creation of the United States; and justified the revolution. The Congress rejected two passages, in which Jefferson had denounced the slave trade and defamed the English people.

Brought into being by the newly created International Red Cross, the Geneva Convention of 1864 was the first international law treaty governing the conduct of nations in wartime, and so marks the origin of modern humanitarian and human rights law. The Convention created provisions for the treatment of sick and wounded soldiers.

The Convention was revised and amended several times, and the current version, approved in 1949 after World War II, comprises four separate conventions. The first and second deal with the care of the sick and wounded in land and maritime warfare; the third deals with the treatment of prisoners of war; and the fourth deals with the protection of civilians and noncombatants. Together, the four Geneva Conventions aim to ensure that human dignity is respected even during hostilities. Their provisions continue to be monitored and enforced by the International Committee of the Red Cross.

The U.N. Charter was signed by 51 nations in the post-war climate of 1945. It established an international organization dedicated to maintaining peace and security and to cooperation in solving economic, social, cultural, and humanitarian problems. Although it affirmed faith in fundamental human rights, its signatories disagreed on the nature of these human rights. The first U.N. conference therefore rejected a proposal to include protection of human rights as an article of the Charter.

The Charter gives the U.N. General Assembly and its Commission on Human Rights primary responsibility for promoting human rights. The Commission was instrumental in creating declarations and covenants on human rights, including civil, political, economic, social, and cultural rights. Although not legally enforceable, these documents are used to interpret the human rights provisions of the U.N. Charter.

Because representatives at the U.N. conference in 1945 wrestled with reconciling their various conceptions of human rights, the clauses relating to human rights that were finally included in the U.N. Charter were very ambiguous. The U.N. assigned a Commission, with Eleanor Roosevelt as chairperson, to clarify the Charter's references to human rights. The result was a statement of universal goals concerning human rights and freedoms, which was adopted by the U.N. General Assembly in 1948. The Declaration is not legally binding, but its content has been incorporated into many national constitutions, and it has become a standard measure of human rights.

Debates over the priority of individuals' political and civil rights versus social and economic rights made drafting the Declaration a long and arduous process. Socialist nations supported primacy of the latter. Many of the eastern-bloc countries abstained from voting; Saudi Arabia objected to religious freedom; and South Africa objected to racial equality.

1989 -International Convention on the Rights of the Child was done, which provide a strong safeguard to the children. Like this many other convictions and agreement has been done till date.

Looking at the concept of Human Rights from a historical perspective, it would be seen that it is neither completely western in origin nor so modern. It is a crystallization of values that are common heritage of mankind. In India references occur as early as in the *Rig Veda* to the three civil liberties of *Tana* (body), *Shridhi* (dwelling house), *jibasi* (life). The reference in vedas about the entire world is one family- *Vasudhev Kutumbkam*—addresses the question of human Rights.

Long before the Indian epic *Mahabharata* described the civil liberty of on individual in an political state. Ancient Indian society was a highly structured and well organized affair with fundamental rights and duties not only of individuals but of classes, communities and castes clearly laid down. The concept of *Dharma,* the supreme law which governed the sovereign and the subject alike covered the basic principles involved in the theory of rights, duties and freedom. Kautilya, the author of the celebrated political treaties *Arthashastra,* not only affirmed and elaborated the civil and legal rights first formulated by Manu but also added a number of economic rights. Comparing Indian situations with other ancient civilizations, Basham writes in *The Wonder That was India*:

"Yet our overall impression is that in no other part of the ancient world were the relations of man and man and of man and the state, so fair and humane. In no other ancient law book are there right so well protected in *Arthashastra.* No other ancient law given proclaimed such noble ideals of fair play in battle as did Manu.... to us the most striking feature of ancient Indian civilization is its humanity.

Fundamental Human Rights in India, in the sense of civil liberties with their modern attributes and overtones are, however, a development more or less parallel to the growth of constitutional government and parliamentary institution from the time of British rule. The recognition, protection and implementation of human rights in the Constitution of India had its genesis in the forces that operated in the national struggle for independence during the British rule.

When the Constitution of India was being framed, the constituent assembly had before it the Bill of Rights, the Universal Declaration of Human Rights and the work on Covenants on Human Rights was in process before the commissions on Human Rights. India being party to UDHR, the constituent assembly shaped Indian Constitution in the light of this declaration and the Covenants on Human Rights which were being drafted.

Naturally, therefore in the Constitution it was finally drafted and adopted, provisions to be found for a broad range of fundamental rights securing the rights of equality, liberty, fair trial, religion and finally, also the right to seek and obtain judicial remedies.

Full enjoyment of all human rights by all in a country depends on their adequate protection under constitution law providing adequate safeguards against any abuse of power and on delivery of justice by an independent judiciary and an efficient and impartial machinery of law enforcement, especially the police. The high courts as well as Supreme Court have therefore been empowered to protect these rights and to declare any executive action or even legislation invalid when found to contravene the fundamental rights. What is more, unlike anywhere in the world, every one weather a citizen or not, has also been given the right to approach the highest court in the country, namely, the Supreme Court of India, even in the first instance if he could satisfy the court that fundamental right(s) had been abridged or threatened.

The basic unit of the Constitution is the individual and it therefore declares certain fundamental rights to individual citizens of India, which are equally applicable to non-citizens.

The preamble of the constitution declares India to be a sovereign, socialist, secular, democratic republic. The power to exercise legal as well as political sovereignty vests with people.

The objective of the Constitution has been to establish an egalitarian society, free from want and hunger, discrimination and exploitation, guaranteeing justice and liberty to all in an atmosphere conductive to their all-round development. To achieve these objectives a pre eminent position has been accorded to the chapter of Fundamental Rights in Part III and Directive Principle of State Policy in Part IV of the Indian Constitution. The value of freedom and equality befitting the dignity of the human individual, made more complete and substantive by ideals of economic and social justice, so eloquently proclaimed by the preamble and elaborated in the Fundamental Rights and Directive Principles of State Policy constitute the foundational principle of the Indian Constitution.

So, the Fundamental Rights guarantee certain rights to the individuals whereas the Directive Principles of State policy give direction to the state to provide some other rights to its people in specified matters. These together constitute the Conscience of constitution.

Let's Understand Certain Laws Relating to Human Rights in India

Projection of Human Rights Act, 1993

The Act provides for the constitution of a national human rights commission, state human rights commission and human right courts for better protection of human rights.

National Commission of Schedule Castes and Scheduled Tribes

Article 338 of the Constitution requires constitution of the national commission for scheduled castes and scheduled tribes for better protections of the rights of the members of SC and ST.

National Commission for Minorities Act, 1992

An Act to constitute a national commission for minorities for better protection of their rights.

Protection of Civil Rights Act, 1995

Under the Article 17 of the Constitution, untouchability is abolished and its practice in any form is forbidden. With this Act, enforcement of any disability arising out of untouchability has been make an offence punishable in accordance with the relevant provisions.

Just and Humane Conditions of Work

The Central Government had enacted Factories Act, 1948; the Mines Act, 1961; the Plantation Labour Act, 1951; and Industrial Employment (Standing Order) Act, 1966 to implement right to secure just and human conditions of work.

Employment of Manual Scavengers and Construction of Dry Latrines (Prohibition) Act, 1993

Fraternity, assuring the dignity of the individual is one of the objects proclaimed in the preamble to the Constitution. Article 47 requires the state to raise the standard of living and improve the health of the people. This Act has been enacted to achieve those objectives.

Immoral Traffic (Prevention) Act, 1956

Article 23 of the Constitution prohibits traffic in human beings. In May 1950, India ratifies the international convention for suppression of immoral traffic in women and girls. This is an Act to give effect to the same.

Dowry Prohibition Act, 1961

This is an Act to prohibit the evil practice of giving and taking of dowry.

Commission of Sati (Prevention) Act, 1987

Sati or burning alive of widows or women is revolting to the feeling of human nature and is nowhere enjoined by any of the religions of India as an imperative duty. This is an Act of effective prevention of the commission of Sati and its glorification.

Child Marriage Restraint Act, 1929

This was enacted with a view to preventing child marriages, namely, marriage to which either of the contracting parties is under the specified age.

Children (Pledging of Labour) Act, 1993

An Act prohibit the pledging of the labour of children and the employment of children whose labour has been pledged.

Orphanages and other Charitable Homes (Supervision and Control) Act, 1960

An Act to provide for the supervision and control of orphanages, homes for neglected women or children and other like institutions and to penalize criminal activities including indulging in such institutions.

Children Act, 1960

An Act to provide for the care, protection, maintenance, welfare, training, education and rehabilitation of children and for trial of delinquent children in the Union Territories.

Child Labour (Prohibition and Regulation) Act, 1986

The Act bans employment of children in specified occupations and processes, lays down a procedure for inclusion in the schedule of banned occupations and processes and regulates the conditions of work of children employment where they are not prohibited from working.

These are some of the Acts made to provide human rights to the people of India. There are many others like this, such as Equal Remuneration Act, 1976; Juvenile Justice Act, 1986; Young Persons (Harmful Publication) Act, 1956; Caste Disabilities Removal Act, 1950; Mental Health Act, 1987; Education as a Fundamental Right, 2009, etc.

The Protection of Human Rights Act was passed by the parliament in 1993. Under the provisions of the Act the National Human Rights Commission, an autonomous body was constituted in 1993. Some very important function has been decided for NHRC. The commission may – inquire into violation of human rights or negligence in the prevention of such violation; intervene in any proceeding involving any allegation of violation of human rights, pending before a court, with approval of such court; review constitutional safeguards for protection of human rights and recommend measures for their effective implementation; visit under intimation of sate government, any jail to study the living conditions of the inmates and make recommendations thereon; review factors that inhibit enjoyment of human rights and suggest remedial measures; study treaties and other international instruments of human rights and make recommendations for their effective implementation; undertake and promote research in the field of human rights; spread human rights literacy; encourage the efforts of non-governmental organizations for the promotion of human rights.

There are some other commissions those working in field of protecting rights of human being. Following are the commission along with their addresses—

National Human Right Commission
Faridkot House, Copernicus Marg,
Cannaught Place,
New Delhi 110001.

National Commission for Scheduled Castes and Scheduled Tribes,
5th Floor, Loknayak Bhawan, Khan Market,
New Delhi 110003.

National Commission on Women
4, Dean Dayal Upadhaya Marg,
New Delhi 110002.

So Finally What Human Right is?

Human rights are rights inherent to all human beings, whatever our nationality, place of residence, sex, national or ethnic origin, colour, religion, language, or any other status. We are all equally entitled to our human rights without discrimination. These rights are all interrelated, interdependent and indivisible.

Human rights are international norms that help to protect all people everywhere from severe political, legal, and social abuses. Examples of human rights are the right to freedom of religion, the right to a fair trial when charged with a crime, the right not to be tortured, and the right to engage in political activity. These rights exist in morality and in law at the national and international levels. They are addressed primarily to governments, requiring compliance and enforcement. The main sources of the contemporary conception of human rights are the Universal Declaration of Human Rights (United Nations, 1948b) and the many human rights documents and treaties that followed in international organizations such as the United Nations, the Council of Europe, the Organization of American States, and the African Union.

The Universal Declaration of Human Rights (1948) sets out a list of over two dozen specific human rights that countries should respect and protect. These specific rights can be divided into six or more families: Security rights that protect people against crimes such as murder, massacre, torture, and rape; Due Process rights that protect against abuses of the legal system such as imprisonment without trial, secret trials, and excessive punishments; Liberty rights that protect freedoms in areas such as belief, expression, association, assembly, and movement; Political rights that protect the liberty to participate in politics through actions such as communicating, assembling, protesting, voting, and serving in public office; Equality rights that guarantee equal citizenship, equality before the law, and nondiscrimination; and social (or "welfare") rights that require provision of education to all children and protections against severe poverty and starvation. Another family that might be included is group rights. The Universal Declaration does not include group rights, but subsequent treaties do. Group rights include protections of ethnic groups against genocide and the ownership by countries of their national territories and resources.

This section try to explain the general idea of human rights by setting out some defining features. The goal here is to answer the question of what human rights are? with a general description of the contemporary concept rather than a list of specific rights. Two people can have the same general idea of human rights even though they disagree about whether some particular rights are human rights.

First, human rights are *political norms* dealing mainly with how people should be treated by their governments and institutions. They are not ordinary moral norms applying mainly to interpersonal conduct (such as prohibitions of lying and violence).

Second, human rights exist as *moral* and/or *legal* rights. A human right can exist as a shared norm of actual human moralities, and a legal right at the national or international level.

Third, human rights are *numerous* (several dozen) rather than few. John Locke's rights to life, liberty, and property were few and abstract (Locke, 1689), but human rights as we know them today address specific problems (e.g., guaranteeing fair trials, ending slavery, ensuring the availability of education, preventing genocide.)

Fourth, human rights are *minimal* or at least *modest* standards. They are much more concerned with avoiding the terrible than with achieving the best. Their dominant focus is protecting minimally good lives for all people (Nickel, 2006).

Fifth, human rights are *international norms* covering all countries and all people living today. International law plays a crucial role in giving human rights global reach.

Sixth, human rights require *robust justifications* that apply everywhere and support their high priority. Without this they cannot withstand cultural diversity and national sovereignty. Robust justifications are powerful but need not be understood as ones that are irresistible.

Which Rights are Human Rights?

This section discusses the question of which rights belong to the lists of human rights. Not every question of social justice or wise governance is a human rights issue. For example, a country could have too much income inequality, inadequate provision for higher education, or no national parks without violating any human rights.

Human rights are specific and problem-oriented (Dershowitz, 2004; Donnelly, 2003; Shue, 1996; Talbott, 2005). Historic bills of rights often begin with a list of complaints about the abuses of previous regimes or eras. Bills of rights may have preambles that speak grandly and abstractly of life, liberty, and the inherent dignity of persons, but their lists of rights contain specific norms addressed to familiar political, legal, or economic problems.

Questions about which rights are human rights arise in regard to many families of human rights. Discussed below are: Civil and political rights; Minority and group rights; Environmental rights; Social rights.

Civil and Political Rights

Most civil and political rights are not absolute. They are in some cases overridden by other considerations and rightly set aside in those cases. For example, some civil and political rights can be restricted by public and private property rights, by restraining orders related to domestic violence, and by legal punishments. Further, after a disaster such as a hurricane or earthquake free movement is often appropriately suspended to keep out the curious, to permit access of emergency vehicles and equipment, and to prevent looting. The International Covenant on Civil and Political Rights permits, suspension of rights during times 'of public emergency which threatens the life of the nation' (Article 4). But it excludes some rights from suspension including the right to life, the prohibition of torture, the prohibition of slavery, the prohibition of *ex post facto* criminal laws, and freedom of thought and religion.

Many international treaties and other instruments guarantee civil and political rights and include a number of provisions specifically addressing the rights of persons with disabilities. The main treaty at the international level is the International Covenant on Civil and Political Rights (ICCPR). In addition, the Convention Against Torture (CAT), and the Convention on the Rights of the Child (CRC) also contain guarantees of civil and political rights, as do the International Convention on the Elimination of All Forms of Racial Discrimination (CERD), and Convention on the Elimination of All Forms of Discrimination against Women (CEDAW). Regional human rights conventions also contain guarantees of civil and political rights.

The ICCPR was adopted by the UN General Assembly in 1966. It requires that all parties 'respect and ensure to all individuals within their territory and subject to their jurisdiction' the rights which the Covenant recognises. The ICCPR covers a range of traditional civil and political rights, often referred to over simplistically as 'negative' rights, enforceable only in relation to the actions of the state. These rights include (amongst others):

- Right to life (Article 6).
- Right to freedom from cruel, inhuman or degrading treatment or punishment (Article 7).
- Right to liberty and security of the person (Article 9).
- Right to be treated with respect for dignity and with humanity, if deprived of liberty (Article 10).
- Right to freedom of movement and choice of residence (Article 12).
- Right to equality before courts and tribunals, and to a fair hearing in any criminal case or law suit; to be presumed innocent until proved guilty if charged with a criminal offence; and, in determination of any criminal charge, to guarantees including the right of every person:
    - to be informed promptly, in detail and in a language the person understands of the nature and cause of the charge.
    - to be tried without undue delay.
    - to be tried in his or her presence, and defend himself or herself in person or through counsel of his or her own choosing.

  - to have legal assistance assigned where required by the interests of justice, free of charge where the person has insufficient means to pay.
  - to examine witnesses.
  - to have the free assistance of an interpreter if he or she cannot speak the language used in court (Article 14).
- Right to recognition as a person before the law (Article 16).
- Right to freedom from arbitrary interference with privacy or family life (Article 17).
- Right to freedom of conscience and religion (Article 18).
- Right to freedom of opinion, expression and information (Article 19).
- Right to freedom of association including the right to form and join trade unions (Article 22).
- Right to marry and found a family (Article 23).
- Right of children to special protection (Article 24).
- Right to take part in public affairs, to vote and to be elected, and to have access on equal terms to public service (Article 25).
- Right of people belonging to ethnic, religious or linguistic minorities to enjoy their own culture, practice their religion or use their own language, in community with other members of their group (Article 27).

Civil and Political Rights in Indian Law

The Constitution of India has privileged civil political rights such as right to life and liberty, equality before the law, freedom of speech and expression, association, religion, etc., by including them as fundamental rights. A number of these rights have been guaranteed for all persons, others can be asserted by citizens only and still others are exclusive to religious and linguistic minorities.

To underscore the primacy of these rights, Article 13(1) provides that "all laws in force in the territory of India before the commencement of the Constitution, in so far as they are inconsistent with the provisions of this part shall to the extent of inconsistency be void." And Clause (2) of the article prohibits the State from making any law which "takes away or abridges the rights conferred by this part and any law made in contravention of this clause shall to the extent of the contravention be void". Rights would just be pious obligations unless remedies are provided. Articles 32 and 226 of the Indian Constitution provide such remedies. Article 32(1) guarantees the right to move the Supreme Court by appropriate proceedings for enforcement of the fundamental rights and to further emphasise on the importance of the remedial mechanism, Clause (4) lays down that "the right guaranteed by this article shall not be suspended except as otherwise provided for by this Constitution". Right to approach the Supreme Court for relief itself has become a fundamental right since it falls under Part III of the Constitution.

The efficacy of the remedial mechanism has been further enhanced by Article 226 of the Constitution which accords power to High Courts to "issue to any person or authority, including in appropriate cases any government, ... directions, orders or writs for the enforcement of any of the rights conferred by part III ..."

On a plain reading of the text of the Constitution, if persons with disabilities belong to any of the groups to whom a right has been guaranteed, they can claim the right. As such persons with disability are not excluded from claiming their rights; at the same time the Constitution does not explicitly prohibit discrimination on the basis of disability as is the case for race, caste, sex, descent and place of birth. This query becomes vital because bearers of civil and political rights are presumed to be autonomous, capable of exercising their capacity before the law and equally enjoy the protection of law. This concept is best articulated in Article 14 of the Constitution, which says, "the State shall not deny to any person equality before the law or the equal protection of the laws within the territory of India." The question remains whether or not persons with disability can exercise their full legal capacity in the absence of explicit protection? This would be examined to some length in the discussion of specific civil and political.

Minority and Group Rights

Concern for the equal rights of disadvantaged groups is a longstanding concern of the human rights movement. Human rights documents emphasize that all people, including women and members of minority ethnic and religious groups, have the same basic rights and should be able to enjoy them without discrimination.

Some standard individual rights are especially important to ethnic and religious minorities, including rights to freedom of association, freedom of assembly, freedom of religion, and freedom from discrimination. Human rights documents also include rights that refer to minorities explicitly and give them special protections. For example, the Civil and Political Covenant in Article 27 says that persons belonging to ethnic, religious, or linguistic minorities "shall not be denied the right, in community with other members of their group, to enjoy their own culture, to profess and practice their own religion, or to use their own language."

Since 1964 the United Nations has mainly dealt with the rights of women and minorities through specialized treaties such as the International Convention of the Elimination of All Forms of Racial Discrimination (1965); the Convention of the Elimination of all Forms of Discrimination Against Women (1979); the Convention of the Rights of the Child (1989), and the Convention on the Rights of Persons with Disabilities (2007). See also the Declaration of the Rights of Indigenous People (2007). Specialized treaties allow international norms to address unique problems of particular groups such as assistance and care during pregnancy and childbearing in the case of women, custody issues in the case of children, and the loss of historic territories by indigenous peoples.

Minority groups are often targets of violence. Human rights norms call upon governments to refrain from such violence and to provide protections against it. This work is partly done by the right to life, which is a standard individual right. It is also done by the right against genocide which protects *groups* from attempts to destroy or decimate them. The Genocide Convention was one of the first human rights treaties after World War II. In Article 2 it gives the following definition of genocide:...

Genocide means any of the following acts committed with intent to destroy, in whole or in part, a national, ethnical, racial, or religious group, as such:

1. Killing members of the group;
2. Causing serious bodily or mental harm to members of the group;
3. Deliberately inflicting on the group conditions of life calculated to bring about its physical destruction in whole or in part;
4. Imposing measures intended to prevent births within the group;
5. Forcibly transferring children of the group to another group.

The right against genocide seems to be a group right. It is held by both individuals and groups and provides protection to groups as groups. It is largely negative in the sense that it requires governments and other agencies to refrain from destroying groups; but it also requires that legal and other protections against genocide be created at the national level.

Can a group right fit the general idea of human rights proposed earlier? Perhaps it can if we broaden the conception of who can hold human rights to include ethnic and religious groups. This can be made more palatable, perhaps, by recognizing that the beneficiaries of the right against genocide are individual humans who enjoy greater security against attempts to destroy the group to which they belong (Kymlicka, 1989).

Environmental Rights

The term environment" is used to refer to everything that is around us: land, water, atmosphere, places of special importance, plant and animal life. The environment therefore has a tremendous influence on human life and the well-being of social communities.

The environment affects us all. We all need a healthy environment to live healthy lives: clean air and water, safe living areas, sufficient and healthy foods. When the environment becomes degraded, it affects us all in the long run, but poor people are the first to suffer.

We all strive for an improved quality of life—now and in the future. We all want our children to have better opportunities and to live healthy and happy lives. For that we need economic development, social justice and a healthy, sustainable environment.

In practice this means that:

- our daily living and working environments must be improved.
- all people must have equal access to land and natural resources.
- we must use social, cultural and natural resources in a sustainable manner.
- we must promote public participation in decisions about how the environment is used.

Environmental rights mean access to the unspoiled natural resources that enable survival, including land, shelter, food, water and air. They also include more purely ecological rights, including the right for a certain beetle to survive or the right for an individual to enjoy an unspoiled landscape.

Our vision of environmental rights include political rights like rights for indigenous peoples and other collectivities, the right to information and participation in decision-making, freedom of opinion and expression, and the right to resist unwanted developments.

We also believe in the right to claim reparations for violated rights, including rights for climate refugees and others displaced by environmental destruction, the right to claim ecological debt, and the right to environmental justice.

Many of these rights, particularly the political ones, are well-established and enshrined in various conventions and agreements. We can credit the establishment of some of these rights, as well as the acceptance of others that are not yet legally recognised, to the ongoing struggles of communities and indigenous peoples around the world.

Other new rights, including rights for climate refugees, have arisen over recent years due to the acceleration of economic globalization and the accompanying environmental destruction and social disruption. Still others, like the right to claim ecological debt, have emerged as the result of years of campaigning by 'Friends of the Earth' and others for the recognition of the impacts of northern resource depletion and natural destruction in southern countries.

All of these rights are equally important, and they are all interdependent. Environmental rights are human rights, as people's livelihoods, their health, and sometimes their very existence depend upon the quality of and their access to the surrounding environment as well as the recognition of their rights to information, participation, security and redress.

In spite of the danger of rights inflation, there are doubtless norms that should be counted as human rights but are not generally so treated. After all, there are lots of areas in which people's dignity and fundamental interests are threatened by governmental actions and omissions. Consider environmental rights, which are often defined as rights of animals or of nature itself. Conceived in this way they do not fit our general idea of human rights because the rightholders are not humans or human groups. But more modest formulations are possible; environmental rights can be understood as rights to an environment that is healthy and safe. Such a right is human-oriented: it does not cover directly issues such as the claims of animals, biodiversity, or sustainable development (Nickel 1993. See also Hayward, 2005).

The right to a safe environment can be sculpted to fit the general idea of human rights suggested above by conceiving it as primarily imposing responsibilities on governments and international organizations. It calls on them to regulate the activities of both governmental and non-governmental agents to ensure that environmental safety is maintained. Citizens are secondary addressees. This right sets out a minimal environmental standard, safety for humans, rather than calling for higher and broader standards of environmental protection. (Countries that are able to implement higher standards are of course free to enact those standards in their law or bill of rights.)

A justification for this right must show that environmental problems pose serious threats to fundamental human interests, values, or norms; that governments may appropriately be burdened with the responsibility of protecting people against these threats; and that most governments actually have the ability to do this. This last requirement—feasibility—may be the most difficult. Environmental protection is expensive and difficult, and many governments will be unable to do very much of it while meeting other important responsibilities. The problem of feasibility in poorer countries might be addressed here in the same way that it was in the Social Covenant. That treaty commits governments not to the immediate realization of social rights for all, but rather to making the realization of such rights a high-priority goal and beginning to take steps towards its fulfillment.

Implementing a new right has opportunity costs. If no new resources are available, implementing a new right will mean that fewer resources are available for the implementation of existing rights. Rights are not magical sources of supply. This is not to deny, however, that successful implementation of a right can reduce threats in some areas and thereby reduce costs. For example, success in protecting the rights of minorities may reduce ethnic conflict and the threats to rights that it generates.

Economic, Social and Cultural Rights

The economic, social and cultural rights are socio-economic human rights, such as the right to education, the right to housing and the right to health. Economic, social and cultural rights are recognised and protected in international and regional human rights instruments. Member states have a legal obligation to respect, protect and fulfil economic, social and cultural rights and are expected to take "progressive action" towards their fulfilment.

Cultural rights should take central place in the consideration of rights issues and the striving towards a more just world order. Such an order would encompass not only distributive justice, but also an inclusive vision that would take cognizance of the many varied expressions of culture as well as an understanding of the inter-dependence of cultural rights in tandem with other human rights.

Yet cultural rights are the least understood and developed of the rights that have been guaranteed under international law. This seeming paradox is due to the complexity of the area and the fact that attention has been given only recently to ESC rights as a whole.

One source of the complexity is the varying understandings of 'culture.' Definitions include:

1. Acquaintance with and taste in fine arts, humanities, and broad aspects of science as distinguished from vocational and technical skills.
2. The integrated pattern of human behavior that includes thought, speech, action, and artifacts and depends upon man's capacity for learning and transmitting knowledge to succeeding generations.
3. The customary beliefs, social forms, and material traits of a racial, religious, or social group.

Each of these definitions is reflected in different provisions of international human rights law. While culture has been addressed in a number of ways in human rights activism—through concern for freedom of expression, freedom of information and the rights of minorities—it is principally culture as described in the second and third definitions that makes the issue of cultural rights complex and difficult.

Our involvement in culture, as a pattern of thought, speech and action, is largely unconscious. From the moment each of us is born, we are raised within a culture. Unless we are exposed in some significant way to other cultures, we rarely develop an awareness of many of the distinctive characteristics of our own culture. They are, for us, simply givens.' There is thus an inherent difficulty in cultural rights: To think about cultural rights, we need to treat consciously something that is largely unconscious for most of us.

Cultural anthropologists tell us that culture is transmitted through a highly complex process comprising a mixture of material and nonmaterial components. Culture can be reflected and expressed through the type of housing we choose to live in and the people with whom we share the housing; the type of food we grow or eat, and how we grow or eat it; the type of music we play or listen to, and how we play or listen to it; the religion we identify with; and the landholding patterns in our society. Culture is reflected in and expressed through our relationships with parents, children, relatives, friends and strangers as well as with other cultures and with the physical world around us.

All of these material and non-material aspects of a culture are infused with values that are transmitted to succeeding generations. Addressing cultural rights can be contentious in part because cultural rights are intimately related to these values—to what we believe is important and what unimportant, what is good and what is bad. Furthermore, in order to understand cultural values in a specific context (and it is difficult to consider cultural values outside of a specific context), it is essential to understand the often subtle differences between cultural values and religious ideas. There is often considerable confusion in determining if an abuse arises from an impingement on cultural rights or on religious rights; the lack of clarity often leads to problems in addressing specific issues. Cultural values are intimately related to our sense of identity. Challenges to our culture thus become challenges to the integrity of each of us as a person and to the values that are closest to our hearts. They threaten our understanding of ourselves and of our world. As a result, challenges to culture generate strong, emotionally charged, survival responses.

Issues of self-identity and self-understanding have traditionally fallen within the domain of the psychologist, sociologist or anthropologist. Except when dealing with the psychological effects of torture or other trauma wrought by human rights abuses, human rights activists have seldom directly addressed problems that arise in this essential yet elusive area of self-identity and self-worth. Ironically, it is this lack of familiarity with and understanding about what makes human beings tick that is one of the central reasons that activism on cultural rights is problematic.

Finally, addressing cultural rights is complex because culture has been historically bound up with questions of power. Throughout human history, dominant cultures in all parts of the world have imposed or tried to impose their own patterns of thought, speech and action on the peoples they have encountered or on weaker members of their own societies. As a result, issues of culture and cultural rights are often associated with historical grievances arising from these impositions.

International human rights law is caught in the conundrum of this history. While the Universal Declaration of Human Rights is a product of the United Nations, whose member nations represent a broad range of cultures, and most of the values represented in the UDHR are shared by cultures around the world, the preponderant powers in the United Nations at the time of the drafting were the western nations. As a result, the UDHR to a large extent embodies the cultural values of those powers. In discussing cultural rights, it thus is necessary to examine industrialization, colonization and the liberation struggles in various parts of the world. The extent to which specific cultural values are the product of these historical circumstances has to be kept in view.

The more recent phenomenon of globalization has also had a deep impact on cultural values. While some aspects of globalization, such as greater access to information, have had liberating effects, the consumption-oriented, materialist pattern of development promoted by globalization has systematically eroded notions of equity. Small communities and indigenous groups have lost a great deal of their traditional knowledge and wealth in the onslaught of a culture of materialism and lopsided developmental priorities adopted by governments all over the world. Globalization has had an adverse impact on the ESC rights of people, especially of the vast majority of the world's poor. Economic rights have traditionally been referred to as part of the second generation of human rights together with social and cultural rights. Indeed, the traditional classification of human rights is as follows:

- The first generation refers to civil and political rights.
- The second generation comprises economic, social and cultural rights.

The third generation refers to collective rights.

Economic rights include the right to work, the right to the free choice of employment and to just and favourable conditions of work; the right to form and join trade unions: the right to strike; the right to social security; and the right to own property.

Contrary to civil and political rights, which are immediately applicable and essentially based on the prohibition of states from doing something (i.e., resort to torture, take actions that curtail freedom of speech, freedom of religion, or the right to vote, etc.), economic rights tend to be considered as requiring states to take action, usually in the form of specific legislation, policies or programmes, so those rights can be realised. The realisation of those rights is seen as progressive: full economic, social, and cultural rights can be achieved only gradually. Resources and time may be required, though international legislation clearly states that full rights should be reached over time, and that states have a legal obligation to take immediate and continued action to do so. Moreover, any action, whether legal or political, taken to diminish existing protections and levels of realisation of these rights should be prohibited.

All human rights are indivisible, inter-dependent and inter-related, and the fulfilment and protection of one right affects that of others. This is true among all rights and among or within specific categories of rights. For instance, economic rights are closely linked to social and cultural rights. The right to work, for example, is connected to that of ensuring minimum standards of living, etc. Just as the distinction between civil and political rights is sometimes blurred, the difference between economic, social, and cultural rights is not always obvious. For example, the right to education has been considered by different experts as an economic, social or cultural right.

In international human rights law, the realisation of economic rights is provided for in Chapter IX of the UN Charter and in the Universal Declaration of Human Rights, the International Covenant on Economic, Social and Cultural Rights (CESCR), the International Labour Organisation, and various regional documents.

The CESCR is monitored by the Committee on Economic, Social and Cultural Rights, which is composed of independent experts appointed by the United Nations. The Committee is responsible for monitoring the implementation of the Covenant by its states parties. They are required to submit regular reports on how they are implementing these rights. Such information is provided through self-reporting and thus may be limited. The reports provided are examined by the Committee, which then elaborates "concluding observations" in which it addresses its potential concerns and recommendations. To date, the Committee is not enabled to consider individual complaints against states parties, though a draft Optional Protocol, under consideration, could provide the Committee with the jurisdiction to do so.

The Social Covenant's list of rights includes non-discrimination and equality for women in the economic and social area (Articles 2 and 3), freedom to work and opportunities to work (Article 4), fair pay and decent conditions of work (Article 7), the right to form trade unions and to strike (Article 8), social security (Article 9), special protections for mothers and children (Article 10), the right to adequate food, clothing, and housing (Article 11), the right to basic health services (Article 12), the right to education (Article 13), and the right to participate in cultural life and scientific progress (Article 15).

Article 2.1 of the Social Covenant sets out what each of the parties commits itself to do about this list, namely to "take steps, individually and through international assistance and co-operation. . . to the maximum of its available resources, with a view to achieving progressively the full realization of the rights recognized in the present Covenant." In contrast, the Civil and Political Covenant simply commits its signatories to "respect and to ensure to all individuals within its territory the rights recognized in the present Covenant" (Article 2.1). The contrast between these two levels of commitment has led some people to suspect that economic and social rights are really just goals.

Why did the Social Covenant opt for progressive implementation and thereby treat its rights as being somewhat like goals? The main reason, I think, is that more than half of the world's countries were in no position, in terms of economic, institutional, and human resources, to realize these standards fully or even largely. For many countries, non-compliance due to inability would have been certain if these standards had been treated as immediately binding. We will return to this topic below.

Human rights, such as rights to freedom from torture or to fair trials in criminal and civil cases, set out extremely important standards that governments everywhere should meet. One might object that social rights do not meet this standard of great importance. Perhaps they identify valuable goods, but not extremely valuable goods. If this objection is that some formulations of social rights in international human rights documents are too expansive it can be conceded and those formulations rejected or qualified. It is far from the case, however, that all or most social rights pertain to superficial interests. To discuss the issue of importance I will use two social rights as examples: the right to an adequate standard of living, and the right to free public education. These rights require governments to try to remedy widespread and serious evils such as hunger and ignorance.

The importance of food and other basic material conditions of life is easy to show. These goods are essential to people's ability to live, function, and flourish. Without adequate access to these goods, interests in life, health, and liberty are endangered and serious illness and death are probable. The connection between having a minimally good life and having reasonably secure access to the goods the right guarantees is direct and obvious—something that is not always true with other human rights.

In the contemporary world lack of access to educational opportunities typically limits (both absolutely and comparatively) people's abilities to participate fully and effectively in the political and economic life of their country (Hodgson, 1998). Lack of education increases the likelihood of unemployment and underemployment.

Another way to support the importance of social rights is to show their importance to the full implementation of civil and political rights. If a government succeeds in eliminating hunger and providing education to everyone this promotes people's abilities to know, use, and enjoy their liberties, due process rights, and rights of political participation. This is easiest to see in regard to education. Ignorance is a barrier to the realization of civil and political rights because uneducated people often do not know what rights they have and what they can do to use and defend them. It is also easy to see in the area of democratic participation. Education and a minimum income make it easier for people at the bottom economically to follow politics, participate in political campaigns, and to spend the time and money needed to go to the polls and vote.

Further, we should not think of social rights as simply giving everyone a free supply of the goods these rights protect. Guarantees of things like food and housing will be intolerably expensive and will undermine productivity if everyone simply receives a free supply. A viable system of social rights will require most people to provide these goods for themselves and their families through work as long as they are given the necessary opportunities, education, and infrastructure. Government-implemented social rights provide guarantees of availability (or secure access), but governments should have to supply the requisite goods in only a small fraction of cases. Note that primary education is often an exception to this since many countries provide free public education irrespective of ability to pay.

Once we recognize that liberty rights also carry high costs, that intelligent systems of provision for social rights supply the requisite goods to people in only a small minority of cases, and that these systems are substitutes for other, more local ways of providing for the needy, the difference in size between the costs of liberty rights and the costs of social rights ceases to seem so large.

Even if the burdens imposed by social rights are not excessive, it might still be wrong to impose them on individuals. Libertarians object to social rights as requiring impermissible taxation. Nozick, for example, says that "Taxation of earnings from labor is on a par with forced labor". This view is vulnerable to an attack asserting two things. First, taxation is permissible when it is used to support government-organized systems of humanitarian assistance that fulfill more effectively than charity duties of assistance that all individuals have. Second, property rights are not so strong that they can never be outweighed by the requirements of meeting other rights.

The third objection to social rights is that they are not feasible in many countries. It is very expensive to provide guarantees of subsistence, minimal public health measures, and basic education. As we saw above, the Social Covenant dealt with the issue of feasibility by calling for progressive implementation, that is, implementation as financial and other resources permit. Does this view of implementation turn social rights into high-priority goals? If so, is that a bad thing?

Standards that outrun the abilities of many of their addressees are good candidates for normative treatment as goals. Treating such standards as goals, which allows us to view them as largely aspirational rather than as imposing immediate duties, avoids massive problems of inability-based non-compliance. One may worry, however, that this is too much of a demotion. As norms, goals seem much weaker than rights. But goals can be formulated in ways that make them more like rights. Goals can be assigned addressees (the party who is to pursue the goal), beneficiaries, scopes that define the objective to be pursued, and a high level of priority. Strong reasons for the importance of these goals can be provided. And supervisory bodies can monitor levels of progress and pressure low-performing addressees to attend to and work on their goals.

Treating very demanding rights as goals has several advantages. One is that proposed goals that exceed one's abilities, not as farcical as proposed duties that exceed one's abilities. Creating grand lists of human rights that many countries cannot at present realize seems fraudulent to many people, and perhaps this fraudulence is reduced if we understand that these rights are really goals that countries should promote. Goals are inherently ability-calibrated. What you should do now about your goals depends on your abilities and other commitments. Goals coexist happily with low levels of ability to achieve them. Another advantage is that goals are flexible; addressees with different levels of ability can choose ways of pursuing the goals that suit their circumstances and means. Because of these attractions of goals, it will be worth exploring ways to transform very demanding human rights into goals. The transformation may be full or partial.

A right together with its supporting reasons might be divided into two parts. One part, call it the demand side, sets out the rightholder's claim and the reasons why it is very valuable or important that this claim be fulfilled. If the right is the right to a fair trial when one is arrested and accused of a crime, the demand side would set out the rightholder's claim to a fair trial and the reasons why that claim is very valuable or important. The other part, the supply side, would set out the addressees' responsibilities in regard to the rightholder's claim. It would explain why this claim to a fair trial is a matter of duty, what the duties are, and why it is these particular addressees rather than other possible addressees that have the duty.

A goal that is similar to a right could also be divided into these two parts. The demand side would set out the beneficiary's claim or demand and the reasons why it is very desirable or important that this demand be fulfilled. For example, the demand side might set out the reasons why it is desirable for the beneficiary to have access to employment. And the supply side would set out the addressee's responsibility in regard to the beneficiary's demand. It would explain why promoting access to employment for the beneficiary should be a goal for the addressee. It does not impose duties on the addressee, but it shows that the addressee has good reasons for acting to satisfy the demand.

Since even a goal that is supported by good reasons imposes no duties that is, fails to be mandatory in character, we may think that such goals are poor substitutes for rights and should not be called rights. But it is possible to create right-goal mixtures that contain some mandatory elements and that therefore seem more like real rights (see Brems, 2009 for a similar idea). A minimal right-goal mixture would include a duty to *try to realize the goal as quickly as possible.* Here the demand side would set out the beneficiary's demand or claim and the reasons why it is very desirable or important that this demand be fulfilled. And the supply side would explain not only why the addressee has good reasons to pursue this goal, but also explain why the addressee has a duty to try to realize this goal with all deliberate speed. The economic and social rights in the Social Covenant seem to fit this model. The countries ratifying the Covenant agree to make it a matter of government duty to realize the list of rights as soon as possible. As we saw earlier, each of the Social Covenant's signatories has agreed to "take steps, individually and through international assistance and co-operation to the maximum of its available resources, with a view to achieving progressively the full realization of the rights recognized in the present Covenant." The signatories agree, on this interpretation, to make it a matter of duty to realize the listed rights as soon and as far as resources permit.

A problem with such a right-goal mixture is that it allows the addressee great discretion concerning *when* to do something about the right and *how much* to do. A body supervising compliance with a human rights treaty may wish to remove some of this discretion by requiring that the addressees at least take some significant and good faith steps immediately and regularly and that these steps be documented. Duties to try are less vaporous if they are combined with duties that require immediate steps. Countries may be required to act in certain ways (e.g., make a good faith effort and be prepared to demonstrate that they have done so), set specific benchmarks and timetables, establish agencies to work on the goals, provide them with budgets, and use expert assistance from international agencies. To facilitate the monitoring of compliance the country may be required to collect data continuously concerning realization of the goals, make periodic reports, and allow its citizens to complain to the monitoring body about failures to pursue the goals energetically (United Nations, 1991).

Article 14 of the Social Covenant imposes a conditional duty in regard to the right to education that was set out in Article 13. It says that countries that "have not been able to secure" compulsory primary education, free of charge, "undertake, within two years, to work out and adopt a detailed plan of action for the progressive implementation, within a reasonable number of years, to be fixed in the plan, of the principle of compulsory education free of charge for all." Compliance with this requirement, which is only present for the right to education, involves planning and setting timetables. Instead of, or in addition to, requiring plans and timetables a goal-right mixture could require immediate compliance with minimal standards. The idea is that minimal provision might be within the capacity of all addressees. For example, countries could be required very soon to provide all children with reading and writing instruction.

These ways of creating right-goal mixtures allow us to see that some rights can be goals while still having enough mandatory elements to be counted as rights in a meaningful sense.

A complementary approach to implementing social rights (and other demanding rights as well) in developing countries emphasizes ability enhancement rather than burden reduction. It seeks to increase the ability of developing countries to implement rights effectively. Possible strategies include using aid to increase the resources available for this purpose, providing education to current and future officials, offering technical assistance concerning the mechanisms of implementation, and battling corruption. Human rights theory needs better accounts of how the rights, e.g., of a Haitian create (moral and legal) duties not just for the Haitian government but also for *(1)* other governments, *(2)* international organizations, *(3)* individuals resident in Haiti, and *(4)* individuals resident in other countries.

John Rawls proposed a duty of liberal democratic countries to aid poor or "burdened" countries. Rawls defines burdened societies as ones that "lack the political and cultural traditions, the human capital and know-how and, often, the material and technological resources needed to be well-ordered" (Rawls, 1999). Rawls holds that well-off countries have a moral duty to assist burdened societies. Unfortunately Rawls does not provide much justification for this claim. In particular he does not use his idea of an international original position to work out how the justification for such a duty would go and what objections it would need to overcome.

A good defense of a duty of well-off governments to assist poor countries in realizing human rights would not automatically impose that duty on the citizens of those well-off countries. But perhaps citizens should share somehow in duties of international aid. One approach to explaining how and why citizens share in these duties involves viewing the citizens of a democratic country as having ultimate responsibility for the human rights duties of their government. If their government has a duty to respect or implement the right to a fair trial, or a duty to aid poor countries, its citizens share in that duty. They are required as voters, political agents, and taxpayers to try to promote and support their government's compliance with its human rights duties. This principle of shared duty is particularly attractive in democratic societies where the citizens are the ultimate source of political authority. This view makes individuals back-up addressees for the duties of their governments.

So human rights are the rights those are with us because we all are human beings. These rights are important to feel a person him/her self with dignity and equal to all respect without any kind of social-political-economical and cultural discrimination.

2

Human Rights Education
An Understanding

In last chapter it was tried to develop a broader understanding about the concept and history of Human Rights. This particular chapter will help you to know and explore the notion and concept of Human Rights Education so that an elaborated understanding can be developed about Human Rights Education.

Human rights education can be defined as education, training and information aiming at building a universal culture of human rights through the sharing of knowledge, imparting of skills and molding of attitudes directed to:

- The strengthening of respect for human rights and fundamental freedoms.
- The full development of the human personality and the sense of its dignity.
- The promotion of understanding, tolerance, gender equality and friendship among all nations, indigenous peoples and racial, national, ethnic, religious and linguistic groups.
- The enabling of all persons to participate effectively in a free and democratic society governed by the rule of law.
- The building and maintenance of peace.
- The promotion of people-centred sustainable development and social justice.

Human rights education involves learning about one's own rights and those of others, but it goes beyond this to include learning that human rights are a shared responsibility with practical consequences for how we live together...

Thus, human rights education is about acquiring not only knowledge but also skills and the ability to apply them; it is about developing values, attitudes and behaviour that uphold human rights but also about taking action to defend and promote them. It involves learning about human rights through the practice of human rights.

The United Nations was created to protect future generations from the curse of war and to reiterate the belief in fundamental human rights, in the dignity and value of the human being, and in the equality of men and women. The end of the Cold War leads us to a single global conception of human rights.

The UN's message is: Know your human rights. People who know their rights stand the best chance of realizing them. Knowledge of human rights is the best defense against their violation. Learning about one's rights builds respect for the rights of others and points the way to more tolerant and peaceful societies.

Vast numbers of people are still unaware of their rights. While laws and institutions could in many cases defend them, people must first know where they may turn for help. The Universal Declaration of Human Rights confirms the nations' commitment to the UN Charter on the promotion and protection of human rights. It is now recognized as one of the most important documents in the history of humankind and can be found in the constitutions of countries that became independent after World War II.

The UN General Assembly recommends that the text be distributed in schools. NGOs are asked to bring it to the attention of their members. How many people have actually read this short, epoch-making declaration? How many know of the International Bill of Human Rights, which consists of the declaration; the International Covenant on Economic, Social and Cultural Rights; and the International Covenant on Civil and Political Rights?

The answer is: very few. NGOs are often the first to bring human rights problems to the attention of the UN and the international community. Schools offer an important means of fashioning a human rights culture, as do research institutions, as they provide in-depth information on specific human rights issues.

Human Rights Education encourages people to:

- internalise and apply rights and responsibilities.
- reflect on historical processes that have prevented the realisation of human rights and analyse current structures and systems.
- critically examine human rights in one's nation, those rights and responsibilities that are most pertinent to a group, community or society apply international human rights standards to local and national realities.
- strengthening of respect for fundamental human rights and freedoms.
- the full development of the human personality and sense of dignity.
- The promotion of understanding, recognition, . . . equality and friendship among.
- the enabling of all persons to participate effectively in a free society.
- the furtherance of activities . . . for the maintenance of peace.

Purpose

The primary functions of the Human Rights Education are to:

- advocate and promote respect for, and observance of, human rights.
- encourage the maintenance and development of harmonious relations between individuals and among the diverse groups in society.

Schools should Adopt the Following Goals

- Teachers should apply human rights to school life and the curriculum.
- Human rights should be the basis of relationships in the classroom.
- Human rights concepts should be taught systematically.
- School rules and disciplinary procedures should be based on fair treatment and due process.
- Schools should promote equality and avoid discrimination on the basis of gender, race or disability.
- Teachers should be encouraged to develop a global perspective.

Human Rights Education Principles

The practice of human rights education is consistent with its purpose. Hence the process of human rights education focuses on strengthening respect for the human rights and dignity of participants, and enabling their full and active participation in the learning process. It is,

- accessible, acceptable, and adaptable.
- learner/participant-centred.
- innovative and adaptable to a wide range of learning environments.
- relevant to the social and cultural context of participants.
- aimed at reflecting on lived experience through a human rights viewpoint.
- encouraging of critical thinking and problem-solving.
- directed toward to the physical, emotional, social, intellectual, spiritual and cultural needs of participants.

Any lesson on the women's suffrage movement, the civil rights movement, or the violation of marginalized group can be a human rights lesson if the teacher encourages students to see universal principles of dignity and equality at stake in these events.

An advocacy group's efforts to address hunger in the community through outreach and legislation can become human rights lessons. A shelter's provision of protection to the homeless or victims of domestic violence can also educate both those who offer services and those who need them. Any day care facility, classroom, or non-profit organization that promotes respect, fairness, and dignity is instilling human rights values, even if they are not identified as such.

Efforts to define human rights education in the 1950s and 60s emphasized cognitive learning for young people in a formal school setting. By the 1970s, most educators had extended the concept to include critical thinking skills and concern or empathy for those who have experienced violation of their rights. However, the focus remained on school-based education for youth with little or no attention to personal responsibility or action to promote and defend rights or effect social change.

The mandate for human rights education is unequivocal: you have a human right to know your rights. The Preamble to the Universal Declaration of Human Rights (UDHR) exhorts "every individual and every organ of society" to "strive by teaching and education to promote respect for these rights and freedoms." Article 30 of the UDHR declares that one goal of education should be "the strengthening of respect for human rights and fundamental freedoms." According to the International Covenant on Civil and Political Rights (ICCPR), a government "may not stand in the way of people's learning about."

So Human Rights Education is much more than a lesson in school or a theme of a day. It is a process to equip people with the tools they need to live lives of security of dignity. Human Rights Education provides you the knowledge and understanding about human rights; it develops an attitude and behaviour respectfully of those rights and also develop the ability and skills to uphold and protect Human Rights.

3

What Exists in Praxis?

In previous chapters we get a good understanding about the concept, development and other concerned aspects of human rights. This particular chapter will help you to understand the perspective from praxis. This chapter will provide a better understanding about the human rights perspective in education and pedagogy. Basically as mentioned in introduction data has been collected from classroom observations and interviews with experts in the field of Human Rights.

The entire chapter is being presented in two parts—Classroom observations and interviews with experts of Human Rights.

CLASSROOM OBSERVATIONS

The analysis of the observations is done on some themes. These themes emerges from the data itself. Idea behind this themetical analysis is to present general trends exists in classrooms

What exists in classes?

Participation of learners (respecting learners' views and experiences)

It was being observed that there was no space for learners' participation in class and that always come in the form of students lack of confidence and hesitation. All classes were teacher fronted or we can say teacher dominating where, there is no space for students experiences. It is very important to provide such space to learn to share their view so that all students can understand concept with deeper understanding. Less participation also led students towards insulting each other because now and than discussion take place in class and in this situation whosoever speak other do not bother, even teacher many times rejected their ideas.

Students participation was only in terms of reading the textbook. Some students were active also and used to ask very relevant question but was being rejected like in a class where democracy is being taught.

"Tr—You never listen carefully in class ok, otherwise it is very simple. (loudly she responded)

S—But we do not rule at all, even we do not know how government works

Tr —*chup karo* what you want to sit in parliament to make rules."

This is not simply rejection of students' participation in classes even it is disrespect of the students and violation of their rights as a students. It is also because it has been and accepted that students know nothing and teacher know all.

Many times teacher said I knew you do not know any thing should not ask question to you. So this kind of atmosphere create hindered in students thinking development and because of this when (very few times) they get chance to speak they talk very laymen thing and do not analyzed critically.

It is to be known that classroom is not teachers' territory where he/she will speak and do whatsoever they want.

Nature of questions asked by the teacher and students

Observation clearly showed that the nature of questions took place from both side are some time very problematic. Least effort has been made by teacher to understand the students question and perspective (lesson democracy). The question asked by teacher in this very much class "How government of India works", is certainly problematic and incomplete, which is very weigh. And if we also keep in mind what and how democracy has been introduced to the class, certainly no one can answer this question properly.

Questions asked by teacher in poverty class were also questionable. Teacher was very confused regarding rural and urban poverty. He responded to students question in a very unclear manner and with full of ambiguity. In this class question was specifically asked by a student, class making fun of him because of his poverty.

Questions and response in next class analyzed are blunders. Teacher was forcing students to think and believe that only parliament make rules and rejected the notion of judiciary (what students saying). Teacher could not make it clear to students that judiciary also make laws. On more questions in this regard in this class teacher was about the said stop asking. Even in class (democracy) teacher said "What you want to sit in the parliament and make rules", such one comment certainly de-motivate students. And it is also the violation of their right to speech.

Empowerment of students

No evidences were found in all the classes where teacher want them (students) to become empowers about their rights. It was also not seen that teacher want students to think critically about the topic is being taught. In lack of such opportunities they can not be empowered citizen. So the culture of silence still exist in classrooms.

Teachers' reactions towards students' socio-economic status

It was also seen that teachers are very careless to be more sensitive about the socio economic status of students. As teacher mentioned that "Yes they (poor people) have nothing with them that is why some time they do stealing. Generally you will find poor people in crime and other antisocial events." (Poverty class). Even teacher was silent when class made fun of one of their classmate. So being sensitive towards such things and events are very important for a teacher and responding like this certainly against the way teacher should respond to the class with full of dignity and with full of respect of learners.

Global perspective

Global perspective means how teacher deal with the content. Teacher generally found suffered with very narrow understanding about the concepts. As we know it is very important to provide an open and wide perspective related to any concept. It was observed that teacher only deal with limited knowledge of the concern field. Such as in a class where 'People struggle and movements' were taught the entire focus was just to deal with what is important for examination point of view. "Why you ask question which are not at all part of your course", has been said by the teachers in the class. So the global perspective about different concept was not being dealt with in the class. Human Rights perspective will say to deal and satisfy the students curiosity. But it was not found in the classes in general. So such understanding which is very narrow and having no global perspective can not facilitate students cognitive development on that particular field of knowledge.

Mode of asking question (tone and way)

It motivates learners the way you ask questions to learners. It was being observed that generally teacher ask question very sarcastic manner such as *tumhe pata to nahi hoga par batao* (you do not know still tell me), such way of asking question will always demotivate learners. This is about the tone and way of asking questions. There is one more dimension, that what kind of question teacher asks. Lesson 'people struggle and movement' (class 10th) teacher asked "tell me the benefits of movement." It is very strange the teacher suddenly ask such question at the beginning of the class without introducing the concept to people struggle and movement. At one stage in the same class only teacher said *jaise ye kisaan visaan andolan karte hai or ye nahi samjhte ki hum nokri wale log itni mahangi sabji or anaj kaise khayenge* (like peasants do movement kind of thing, but they do not understand that how we people those are in services will get vegetables and grains). Such kind of question develop a biased attitude towards a community and it is purely against human rights. It also develop low self concept of children belongs to that particular community.

Reflection based dialogue by teacher

Reflection in teaching-learning process not only facilitate the learner but even equally beneficial for teachers. It provide space to think back and ahead about the processes we dealt or will be dealing with. It also make us very analytical. But it was being observed during observation that teacher are not giving space for reflection. We can say this because what they taught in the last class, they just simply add on to that. They do not try to reflect open what they did in the last class, such way of teaching create problem in learning processes. If a teacher do reflection he should be able to be more humanistic to the learning processes. But unfortunately reflection is missing in our school system.

Facilitative attitude

Teacher as a facilitator can provide a better environment for learning and can create a different kind of supportive culture, where learners can learn with understanding and respecting each others way of thinking. But it was being observed that teacher are working in school just to do the job, though we all agreed that teachers' job is more than merely a job. They hardly bother what they said very loosely to the learners. They even do not think how they are treating students. Some time they do partial behavior in term of asking questions and giving opportunities to the learners. Some time they do labeling like *nikkame* (a person having nothing to do) etc., such behavior does not show the evidence of being a good facilitator for students. Their basic idea is just to provide all information to the learner. They need to understand that there is need to motivate the learners instead mugging up them only with information.

Discipline

Most of the teachers viewed discipline in terms of military rules. Like student should be silent in the class, there should not be any noise in the class, students should respect teachers etc. None of them thinking about self discipline and self regulation. If everything is given than how can we expect that discipline will not be given? With this understanding teacher believe teaching-learning process need to take place in discipline and discipline means what, as they (teachers) say. So the normal behaviors which teacher expect from learner also need a rethinking. Researches shows, when there is scope for talking in class, learners understand that concept in more comprehensive way.

It is compulsory for students to stand-up when teachers enter in class. This particular expected behavior is very problematic. And schools are following it just because they believe that it means discipline. So there is a lot of scope to rethink about the discipline with relation to school and also in classrooms.

Extra responsibilities on teachers

It was also being observed that, accept teaching there are many tasks a teacher has to do. Teachers say, they do not get time to think about creative way of teaching. Schools some time do not fill all vacancies like librarian, lab in-charge etc. So a teacher has to do his work well. And in such situation teacher get an excuse not to put more efforts in teaching. We all believe that sufficient time is needed to prepare a class. So it is important that teachers should get sufficient free time to be ready for their classes. Generally it was being observed that they are just rushing from one class to another.

Teaching methods

Researches show that using of multiple methods in teaching provide more space to learner to learn, but it was being observed that generally teacher used only lecture method. Hardly any other method was being used in class. Lecture method itself has inherent domination of authority and provide one way communication, which is very unfair to the students.

Pressure of syllabus completion

One of the basic reason for failing to include human rights perspective in teaching-learning process which came across was the pressure of syllabus completion. Teacher mentioned that there is large content to deal with and we have very less time, so in such a situation it is very tough for us to provide more space for free learning. They accept that, if there is no pressure of syllabus completion they can do better, what they are doing now. These and there many other issues came out from the analysis of the classroom observation. But, question is that how to deal with all these issues. May be issues are less in number but their seriousness is really very serious. Now the time has come to deal with all these problems and issues, but how? Next part of this chapter will help to know you what experts think about human rights and its implication to pedagogy.

WHAT EXPERTS' THINKS?

To have a better understanding about Human Rights and using its perspective in pedagogy. Interviews were being conducted with experts in this area only. Their views really support the work. Experts who were interviewed were:

Dr. Sanjay Dubey
Director
National Human Rights Commission,
New Delhi

Prof. Nalini Juneja
National University for Education Planning and Administration,
New Delhi

Dr. N. Sukumar
Department of Political Science
University of Delhi
Delhi

Their views have been thematically organized and being presented here.

What is their perspective about Human Rights

Nalini Juneja (Prof. in NUEPA) underlined the HR perspective in UNO contexts. She indicated Human Rights as a broad concept. It deals with all aspects of a person throughout his/her life. On the basis of her experiences, she stated that there are lots of human rights related issue exists and she is trying to explore the possibilities to resolve these issues and for this, working from NUEPA. Many times she has talked to the policy-making people in education about the inclusion of Human Rights. In all her work HR plays a pioneer role.

Her special urge is that, all people of society must be aware about their Human Rights and not only need to be aware, instead they also should have such empowerment so that they can use their right without any fear, and can live a life like other human beings. She believes that the understanding of human rights can be enculturate in learners from very early age in term of respecting their need and desire. Institutions like schools can strengthen such processes more.

During discussion it came that she is working specifically to abolish the corporal punishment for children in school and in general. Through such a way, we can dismiss the distinction between theory and practice with special reference to human rights.

Dr. N. Sukumar accepts human rights as a right of day to day life. It is totally based on right to live. It is also related to fundamental rights of a person provided by the established law. His is very concern is that there is no any development in remote areas, then how and what can we even think about their human rights and how can we assume about their applicability. In this condition, it is necessary to promote and establish such organization which can make sure to protect and to maintain their Human Rights. They create social consciousness in them and this consciousness can make them more aware about their rights and can set-up some democratic values. He also showed his concern about encouraging social justice and national unity and the basic assumption behind this idea is global concept of humanism. Every culture and society has their different ways, norms etc., for operating there life and so the notion of rights are also not absolute, it has a very significant context. It is our duty to respect these rights.

The concept of *Vasudhave Kutumbakam,* European renaissance and enlightenment are the glory of development of humanity and all these, considered a persons individuality on priority. He said the human right concept enforce the real capacity and dignity of a person and because of this reason all documents related to human rights include and emphasis the dignity of human being. And if education can include this perspective, then we can be in a different situation altogether in this globalize world.

Director of NHRC (National Human Right Commission), Sanjay Dubey said that human right concept is related very close of dignified life of human beings. In human rights context, life of human should be different from animals. This dignify life is related to various need and demands as a human being for our development like right to live, right to speak, right to be respected, rights to be treated equally etc. These all liberties will create or develop more egalitarian societies and such societies will be fuller of tolerance and peace.

We have been fighting and struggling for our human rights. Struggle to be equal in all terms (political, social and economical) is inseparable part of the history of human development and even now some way of other we all are struggling for our rights but still we find many difficulties to use our rights in practicality. Violation of human rights is not stopped, moreover it exists in different forms and it is going to be more complex day by day.

Elite group of society deliberately wants to maintain this gap, so that a kind of pressure can be forced on other groups of the society. And this deliberate practice creates stratification in societies. Such elite group makes other people to think that they are lower in the societal hierarchy. They use education also as tool or means to establish their monopoly and hegemony. He said but if we can improve our education system certainly we can think to have a more egalitarian society.

What they mean by Pedagogy

Pedagogy is to some way or other includes teaching-learning-process. Nalini Juneja talked about pedagogy with special reference to constructivism, where learner is in the center and teacher works like as facilitator. Teacher supports the learners to enhance the processes where they construct their own knowledge. She said if we provide appropriate environment to a seed, it will grow at its best. The same ways we need to provide a better ways or opportunities to the learners to develop their self.

Generally teaching includes just transfer of knowledge. Where, someone says, the other listen, like news bulletin and only do bombarding of information. What is the necessity and importance of the content or the way we are dealing with our learners, that never has been taken very seriously by the teachers and other school concerned people.

So, it becomes very necessary to provide space to teachers for proper training. There is a great need to think about all these concerns. She has given the example of 'Mirambika School' in this context, how students learn in free environment and so they develop the feel of self responsibility and take interest in studies. So she considered Mirambika system very good.

N. Sukumar says pedagogy is a tool which is related to the over all objectives of education. It depends on teachers nature that how much freedom student can celebrate in classrooms to be satisfied with reference to their curiosity. According to human rights perspective, it is necessary to deal with more enthusiastic approach in classroom. Teacher is a practitioner to improve him/her self and a role modal for his/her students. It is necessary for a teacher to influence students for practical aspect of education. Learners' family environment has very important place for this practical aspect of education. So, it should be started from learner's family. Family is the actual place where socialization of child starts. To ensure the success of this effort, it is important that parents should also be involved in this entire process so that they can facilitate to create free environment at house for children's development. It is essential to realize the parents that these are their rights and duties to collaborate with school in this regard.

Sanjay Dubey emphasise that the role and basic objective of pedagogy is to implement the curriculum. Education and education system is the reflection of any country. He believes that our education system is also human centered and also to some extent include human rights perspective in education policies. But he also stated that there is no much difference in what existed before fifty years and now. He said situation is more serious and problematic now, as many laws has been constituted but there is very less possibility to make them applicable. The gap between theory and practice with relation to human rights is increasing day by day. He said we (NHRC) always try to fill this gap. So that a better mechanism can be developed.

What can be possible relationship between Human Rights and Pedagogy?

Nalini Juneja emphase is the identity of learner as a community and individual. She stated that constructivist ideas of pedagogy is directly related to human rights. But it is still subject of prove. This process will help us to know its merits and demerits, which will help us to make a better relationship between constructivist pedagogy and human rights perspective. She said it is important to improve physical infrastructure, sports, teaching-learning environment in schools. In this regard she also talked about adolescents and school. She stated, there should be the proper way of dealing with the student in this age, as this stage is very crucial. There should be appropriate opportunities to develop their interests. Over burdens should be removed in consideration of human rights. All students should be respected equally, their should not be any kind of discrimination in terms of caste, class, religion, region, gender etc. It is also important to develop self discipline in school and that environment must lead to the healthy relationships between teachers and students.

N. Sukumar also emphasise to develop a friendly relationship between learner and teacher. Power relationship in teaching-learning process discourages the dialogue and sensitivity should be the core of the dialogue. Such dialogue should be two way process. How to respect a student's dignity during interaction is the first thing a teacher should know because dignity of a person is directly related to self respect. And all this is possible only in a friendly environment, where, there is no pressure, only self regulation is active. In this regard he stated that, "If I don't give you free space to interact with me then how these experiences will be communicated and you will also not feel comfortable."

Further he relates the fundamental rights with Human Rights in day to day life. He believes that, it is very important to make human rights an inherent part of education (curriculum). He also emphasise that pedagogy is also need to be changed according to the curriculum and for this it is also important the teacher should encourage students to ask questions, to think critically about current issues, to think them reflectively. He was in favor of having some physical arrangement in school where students can keep their vies in writing as a records. These works can be there in school as archives.

Sanjay Dubey, in this regard said that human rights should be one of the strong premises of entire education system and curriculum. Peace education and environment education should also be included in curriculum. Pedagogy also should be humanistic approach based which provide opportunities to learners to learn in practical terms. Teachers also have to show their commitment in teaching processes through their behaviour. He also stated that every day we are generating new theories but as long as applicability is concern nothing is taking place. He also touched the development of corporatism in Indian and how it is creating problems in development.

Further he related human rights with education. He emphasized that human rights should be included as a compulsory part upto secondary level school enunciation and optional at higher secondary level.

He said it is essential to create an environment to increase knowledge, values, tendency and skill fully based on human rights perspective and for this we have to develop the culture of democracy. Our nation is full of diversities so this task become little more difficult. But educational institution can play a major role in this regard. NGOs are working very effectively in this field to promote and protect human rights. Overall he said, educational institution has a great role to play with reference to the development of human rights.

Notion of Human Rights: India *vs.* Western

Nalini Juneja describe the HR as a Global theory. She said that according to Universal Declaration of Human Rights, rights are of every person and it is important the all human beings can use their rights without any pressure and fear so that they can be developed at their best in all aspect like social, economical and political. It is compulsory to create such situations that always protect their dignify life and this can be achieved if we will achieve universalization of education.

N. Sukumar also emphasis on human rights as a global concept. He also said that to establish peace and democracy an universal collaboration is needed. Further, he underlines the role of many organizational bodies to maintain and revive the peace and democracy. Such organization need to show their cooperation. These may include NGOs, different communities of professionals (including government and private). This collaboration will leads us to a differed world.

He said every society has some culture specific problems in the form of rituals, traditions etc. but we have to deal all these issues under one umbrella that is called human rights.

Sanjay Dubey also emphasized the global concept of human rights. He again emphasized that there should be some determinant factors to make an uniformity between theory and practice specially in India. Though he also accept that discrimination is taking place throughout the world and there is a need for change but for this there is need of active actions. His more emphesis was on to dismiss the gap between theory and practice.

Authority of learner in classroom

According to Nalini Juneja, this depends on the teacher in which role he/she is presenting him/her self in classroom. If he/she is working as a facilitator, there will be more space for students to participate in classroom practices otherwise class will be teacher fronted and teacher dominated. Discipline plays a major role in such situation. Such classroom will be called non-permissive. On other hand there are situation when teacher provide enough space to participate. Such classes will be called as permissive. She said some time it happen that blackboard of the class is very poor and students are not able to read what is written on it, and if they come ahead to note it down then it become indiscipline in teacher' s view. So we also need to redefine the meaning of discipline, what we mean with discipline in a classroom. But she also emphasized on more important aspect that poor teachers are the easiest target of all of us. There is great need to change in policies, about which we are not bothering much.

N. Sukumar emphasized on authority of children in classroom for their creativity. Role of teacher has to create curiosity in children to know about their interest and then provide opportunities to develop them. It largely depends upon teachers nature what kind of authority they provide to the learners? How he behave with students? All these processes will generate the environment in classroom where a student has to work. He also said, students authority also depends on the strategies a teacher uses in the class. If those strategies are teacher dominated then how can we expect learner to participate. So student authority is subject to the nature of teacher and over all environment of the class including pedagogy. But ideally there should be enough space for learner to interact with the teacher and peer group. It means he emphasized the dialogue in the class. Environment which does not promote dialogue will not be able to encourage learner to learn actively.

Role of teacher is as a facilitator in this process. Teachers provide assistance to create knowledge and put learner in teaching learning processes. This process will facilitate them to think creatively and originally. Such environment provides better opportunity to develop a better personality all together.

Human Rights and Right to Education

Nalini Juneja said the basic premises of RTE (Right to Education) is the theory of constructivism, where teacher is in a role of facilitator and students construct their own knowledge and respect their views and ideas.

RTE is talked about the education for all within the age of 6 to 14. She appreciate that effort and said it is a great step in favor of human right. But she also talked about many loop wholes of this bill, such as ignorance of neighbor hood school, disability Act related issues and all.

She said, for some time it has been seen that due to punishment students are taking school as a jail. They do not feel comfortable there. She also relate RTE with teachers authority. She also raise the issue of quality education with special reference to RTE. As teacher has to do many other work accept teaching, students can not be detained before class eighth than what are they learning is very questionable as they also know they can not be failed before class eighth. She also talked about infrastructural problem in school like lack of ramps for physically challenged student, so the effort to make school education inclusive is just a formality. Lots of work needs to be done to implement this bill with full will.

With this she also admitted that after RTE, corporal punishment has been reduced. Other issues are still exists. Some time teacher doesn't care about their way of behaving and talking and that impact students. Children take it very seriously and effecting with low self esteem, lack of confident etc.

In such situations, the goal of free and compulsory education will not be able to reach to the needy people of the society, though RTE deals with human rights perspective but its needs lots of improvement and modifications. Not only RTE even many other education commission reports and education policies are also enforcing human rights perspective.

According to N. Sukumar, as education is the source of knowing about once rights, so RTE is directly related to empowerment of people about their human rights. Implementation of RTE will also facilitate in promoting human rights and the notion of human rights will become more institutionalized. When we try to locate the data at world level, we find that a lot of number of children are out of schooling system. More than half of such children in all-over the world are part of South Asian countries, i.e. Bangladesh, Pakistan, India etc., and out of this population, almost one-third is only in India. Thus, a huge number of children of India are out of schooling system.

It is also a important fact to know that poverty and education is closely related in country like India. Data shows, children of marginalized section in terms of economy are out of the school in larger number. Bihar, Orissa, Assam are some of the examples of low literacy. Due to lack of economic development, the condition of education is also affected very badly. Whatever number attends the school, is also based on gender inequality. Socially discriminated behaviour toward students is also playing a major role for wastage and stagnation. So, this is very clear that the drop out is more of children belong to socially lower caste and class and with them on the basis of gender. Such environment do physical and mental exploitation of learners and become cause of depression etc., and ultimately children leave the school they remaind there in the school because of some reason or other they indulge themselves in anti-social activities.

So first requirement is to create such environment which is free from all kind of discrimination specially based on colour, caste, sex, religion and language. In such situation it will be very easy to implement RTE with human rights perspective.

According to Sanjay Dubey, RTE is a fundamental right in itself. It will be tough task to implement RTE in current situation, where, there is lack of political will. We can think its success on the basis of para teachers. The concept of para teachers itself is a very serious problem in Indian education system. So putting issues like para teacher aside we can not achieve anything. Dichotomy is that government now showing lack of funding to implement this law, in this consideration the whole process (RTE) looks like a political agenda.

What and which type of relationship should be between education and society, is always being a debatable issue among sociologists and educationists still we are struggling with it. A fact that education is an important cognitive tool of a state, which develop and govern by the rulers as they want to maintain their hegemony. So in this context if we will even achieve the goal of RTE still the question of being humanistic (human right perspective) is subject to be investigated. So NHRC is fully committed to make the following more effective:

1. To apply Human Right.
2. To develop Humanistic Environment.
3. To improve mental and cultural preparation of citizen.

Overall, experts share their valuable ideas with us regarding their understanding about human right and how to include it, not only in pedagogy moreover in entire education system. Their views are all together common in favor of promoting and protecting of human rights with special reference to education.

Next unite will facilitate you to understand how to make a classroom human rights perspective based. Analysis also shows that students are completely unaware about their rights and responsibilities, so it has become very important to provide some opportunities to them to explore this area. So with this understanding, next unite is dealing with the some activities including worksheets to make students educated in human rights. There is no such content and textbook for student to read, here only some worksheet and cooperative strategies has been suggesteds, those can facilitate students to be familiar with the concept of human rights. Further next unite overall will develop an understanding about how to use human rights perspective in pedagogy.

UNIT TWO

What is the Need?

Last unit provide us an insight what all exists in classes and teachers and expert views with respect to human rights. this unit will help you to know what all is needed to make a class more human rights perspective based. The entire analysis shows that hardly the notion of human rights perspective exists in pedagogy. so the solutions can not be suggested just to say do this in class and it will happen. A deep and broader understanding based mechanism is needed to make a class human rights based class. It was also observed the students are also very unaware about their every day rights and responsibility. So an actively particpatory program is needed for school system. Suggesting on only in terms of pedagogy will be half effort. With this understanding this unit has for chapters.

4

Teaching about Human Rights

To Know, What You Know

As mentioned above, it was clearly seen that students are not aware about their rights and responsibilities and that is why they become indiscipline, uncritical, unorganized with behavioral aspects. They also do disrespect of their colleague in many ways. So it is essential to help them to know and develop a positive and progressive attitude and understanding about their human rights and responsibilities. For this purpose this chapter will suggest some important content and their pedagogy with relation to Human Rights. This section is a kind of module to facilitate learner as well as teachers, which is based on some useful activities and worksheets. The entire module is containing all together nine lessons. Let's understand about these lessons and apply in our classes.

Brief Introductions of the Lessons

Lesson One

WHAT IS RIGHT WHAT IS WRONG?

This lesson is a starter for students to think about what is right and what is wrong instead just starting with the formal concept of human rights. This develop a sense of feeling towards the system, peer, teachers etc. Also help them to be critical and analytical.

What to do	Will get chance to learn
Why your home rules are not correct?	Reasons for being right and wrong critically.
What will you do to stop their implementation?	Participation and active role-play against unfairness.
What kind of rules you want at your home?	Analytical thinking to think something new.

Lesson Two

HOW HUMAN RIGHT CAME

Student will get chance to know the history of human rights. How does it come in existence? What are international and national document those provide and talk about our human rights. Lesson will also explore, what are good things associated with human rights

What to do	Will get chance to learn
What are human rights?	Explain human rights in their own words and experiences.
Human rights came from	Understand the origin of hunan rights.
How human rights make you feel happy and good?	Feel the beauty to know having human rights.

Lesson Three

DO YOU KNOW WHAT YOUR RIGHTS ARE?

This lesson provides opportunities to learners to explore, what are their rights as a child and as a human being.

What to do	Will get chance to learn
What human rights do you have?	Awareness about their human rights.
What human rights do we all have?	Elaborate the concept of rights with reference to all human beings.
Are human rights important?	Understand and reflect why rights are important.

Lesson Four

HUMAN RIGHTS IN INDIA

This Lesson provides the understanding about the rights Indian Constitution talk about. Lesson will provide them opportunities to understand the relationship or commonality between fundamental rights given by Indian Constitution and UDHR. Lesson also has space to present views about human rights confidently.

What to do	Will get chance to learn
What rights our constitutional preamble provides us	Analyze the preamble of Indian Constitution with respect to rights.
Fundamental rights and universal declaration of human rights	Compare the fundamental rights with universal declaration of human rights.
Read, think and speak	Presentation in an articulated manner.

Lesson Five

RIGHTS FOR ALL

This lesson will facilitate to understand that we all are equal and should be treated equally, whether we are children, women, men, special need children, minorities or dalit. Lesson will help to develop a sense of knowing and respecting everyone's rights.

What to do	Will get chance to learn
What are your rights as children?	Awareness about children's rights.
Do women have same rights as men?	Understand the notion of equality between men and women.
Am I not like other?	Know and feel the discrimination exists within society for different people.

Lesson Six

DO YOU KNOW WHAT YOURS AND OTHERS RESPONSIBILITIES ARE?

This lesson deals with the notion, that human rights can not sustain alone, it is important in the sense that responsibility also should move with it. This lesson will help to facilitate learner to understand some agencies who to protect the human rights. In short, what are our responsibilities and what are government responsibilities.

What to do	Will get chance to learn
Who Protect our human rights?	Understand different agencies who protect our human rights.
How can you make sure that your and others human rights are protected.	Develop a sense of responsibility to respect towards ones own and others rights. Explore the possibilities regarding, how to protect our human rights.

Lesson Seven

ARE WE ALL DIFFERENT OR SOMETHING IS COMMON?

This lesson specifically will talk about the problems and benefits of diversities in a country like India. It will also help to develop a positive attitude towards solving such issues. Lesson will provide space to learn how to respect others perspective irrespective of anything.

What to do	Will get chance to learn
Can you think in what ways you are different from others?	Understand the notion of diversity.
Can you think what commonalities you have with others?	Explore the notions of possibilities for unity in diversity.
What are the common values for all ?	Develop a sense of consciences.

Lesson Eight

WHERE ARE THE PROBLEMS AND POSSIBILITIES?

This lesson will deal with some important issues related to human rights. It will provide space to share learner's ideas and experiences with respect of human rights violation. They will also get chance to relate their own role in promotion of these rights. Will also get chance to reflect, are they doing something wrong with respect to human rights?

What to do	Will get chance to learn
Why we do wrong to others?	Analyse situations critically.
Any experience where you feel you did wrong to some one. Did you realize and feel uncomfortable later?	Reflect upon the past experiences.
What we should do, if we do wrong to some one?	Think analytically for solutions.

Lesson Nine

RETHINKING ABOUT RIGHTS

This lesson will provide space for learner to show and use their creativity on the basis of whatsoever they have explored about human rights till now. They will talk about what are other areas and field in which they want to know human rights. The area of interest may be anything. Also they will be developing guidelines for the improvement in the present course.

What to do	Will get chance to learn
What else except this course you want to learn and understand about human rights.	Analyse critically and reflectively the entire course they have gone through.

Lesson One

WHAT IS RIGHT WHAT IS WRONG?

This lesson presents the concept of human rights with very simple way from their daily life activities. It is providing opportunity to learners to think creatively about their surroundings with the help of a very good activity where they will get chance to know what is right and what is wrong and the reason behind that. This lesson will help them to develop their ability to think analytical.

"Nothing is Right and Nothing is Wrong"

What to Do

- Why your home rules are not correct?
- What will you do to stop their implementation?
- What kind of rules you want at your home?

Will Get Chance to Learn

- Reasons for being right and wrong critically.
- Participation and active role-play against unfairness.
- Analytical thinking to think something new.

What We Need to Facilitate them with

Worksheet 1.1	—	What comes first in your mind?
Resourcesheet	—	New rules list for home.
Worksheet 1.2	—	What rules you find problematic and why?
Worksheet 1.3	—	What rules you want to make for your home?

How to Deal with Class with these Resources

To make them comfortable ask students to draw or write in given worksheet what comes in their minds when you say rights. Let them freely complete this task within 5 minutes. Collect all worksheets (worksheet 1.1). Ask some of them randomly why they made what they have made.

After this initiation, distribute resource sheet to the students. You may use power projector or separate sheet for all students. Let them read this resource sheet and then make pairs. Try to do this in fifteen minutes.

When you feel sufficient time has been given, distribute worksheet 1.2 and ask student to fill it up in pairs after discussion. This will facilitate their collaborative work spirit. A very good thinking process will take place among students, because they have to substantiate their answer with reasons. Provide all together 15 minutes for this.

Pick any worksheet and ask students to elaborate about there decision about rules and reasons. Pick some worksheets (as time permits).

Distribute worksheet 1.3 and ask students to fill it up separately. They will be writing what kind of rules they want for their homes and why. Such an exercise will help them to think analytically.

Note

Summaries at the end of the class if you feel it is needed. You may also leave them without any conclusion.

WORKSHEET 1.1

What comes first in your mind? (Write or draw)

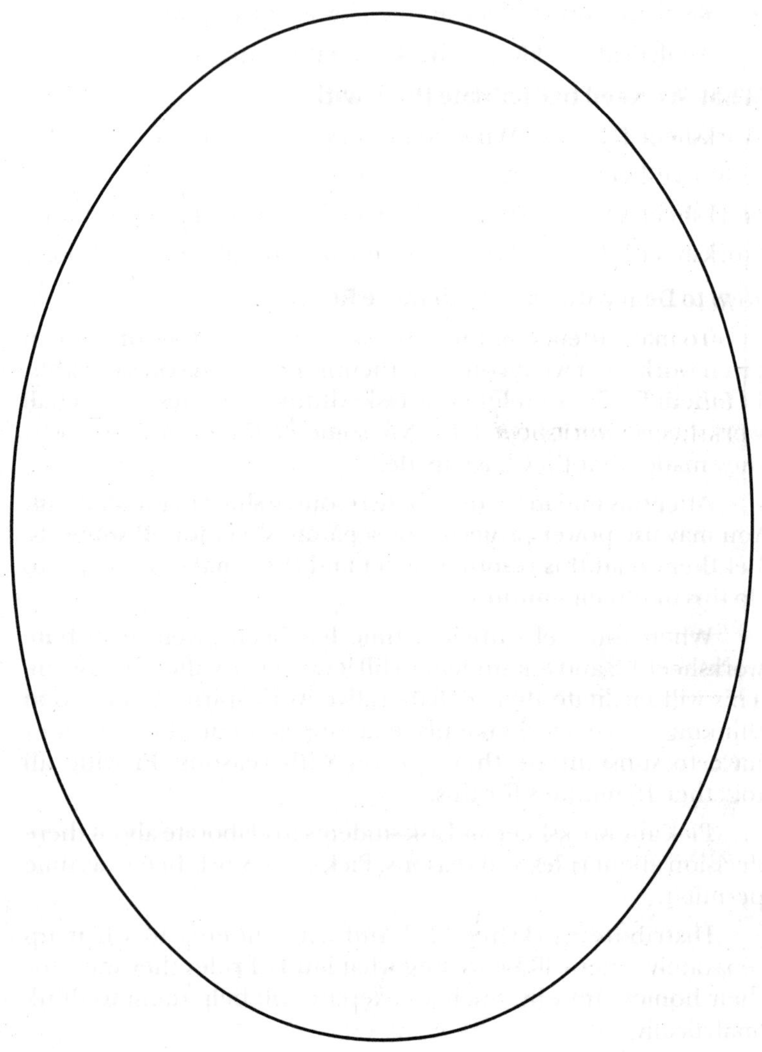

RESOURCE SHEET 1

New Rules for Home

Rule one
All have to wake up by 5 am

Rule two
No breakfast after 7:30 am

Rule three
All will wash their own clothes

Rule four
Nobody can criticize the rules, if do, will be punished

Rule five
No television for children at all.

Rule six
Parks are not safe these days. No play in parks for girls and boy have to come back from park by 5 pm.

Rule seven
If any child will commit mistake, will be punished

Rule eight
No dinner if homework is uncomplete.

Can you think?

Which rules are fair and which are unfair?

Why and why not?

WORKSHEET 1.2

Read the given Resource

Sheet and write the rules you feel are fair or unfair. Also support your answers with reason. You are also allowed to do miner changes in the rules.

Rules	What is your opinion with reason
Rule one All have to wake up by 5 am	
Rule two No breakfast after 7:30 am	
Rule three All will wash their own clothes	
Rule four Nobody can criticize the rules, if do, will be punished	
Rule five No television for children at all.	
Rule six Parks are not safe these days. No play in parks for girls and boy have to come back from park by 5 pm	
Rule seven If any child will commit mistake, will be punished	
Rule eight No dinner if homework is uncomplete.	

WORKSHEET 1.3

Develop some rules for your home those you feel are fairer. And also write why you feel they are fairer?

Rules you want	Why you want
Rule one	
Rule two	
Rule three	
Rule four	
Rule five	
Rule six	

Lesson Two

HOW HUMAN RIGHT CAME ?

In this lesson learners will explore the origin of human rights in a form of story, which will be interesting to them and will involve them in learning processes. They will become familiar with certain national and international documents related to human rights. They will also get chance to know what human rights are, they will explain in their own language. Lesson will also facilitate them to learn and feel the importance and beauty of Human Rights.

"Was there any time when there was no human rights"

What to Do

- What are human rights?
- Human rights came from.
- How human rights make you feel happy and good?

Will Get Chance to Learn

- Explain human rights in their own words and experiences.
- Understand the origin of hunan rights.
- Feel the beauty of having human rights.

What We Need to Facilitate them

Resource Sheet 2	—	History of human rights (very brief in terms of the period and basic characteristics of that period).
Resource Sheet 3	—	Preamble of universal declaration of human rights.
Resource Sheet 4	—	Including some pictures showing violation of human rights.
Worksheet 2.1	—	List out, what kind of problem you can identify?
Worksheet 2.2	—	What are your. rights in school, home and society.
Worksheet 2.3	—	Mention some situations when you feel very happy.

How to Deal with Class with these Resources

Provide the Resource Sheets 2 and 3 to the learners and provide 5-10 minutes to go through the sheet. Though this resource sheet is not specifically for their learning the dates and name of conviction. This resource sheet is only to familiarize them with the short history of human rights. Teacher need to tell them very short story about the conviction given in list.

After their familiarization with the small history of human rights, distribute Resource Sheet 4 to the learners. It contains some picture showing violence of human rights. Ask students to think about this picture for some time. Then after ask them to present their views with class.

Now distribute Worksheet 2.1 and ask them to fill it up on the bases of Resource Sheet 4. They will be writing the problems they saw in the pictures. Teacher may use other picture than suggested here.

After that provide them Worksheet 2.2 and provide them enough space to think and write the worksheet. They will get chance to explore their daily life and will relate it with their rights. They will do it in three categories— school, home, and society. Collect worksheet 2.2 and make chart for class out the worksheet and put on bulletin board. (Teacher is suppose to make that chart next day).

Finally provide Worksheet 2.3 to the learners. Ask them to share some experiences of when they feel very happy and enjoy. After that teacher may relate their views to explain why rights are important.

RESOURCE SHEET 2

c. 1750 B.C.E.	—	Code of Hammurabi, Babylonia.
c. 1200 - c. 300 B.C.E.	—	Old Testament.
c. 551 - c. 479 B.C.E.	—	Confucius - "Do unto others what you wish to do unto yourself."
1215	—	Magna Carta, England.
1689	—	English Bill of Rights, England.
1776	—	Declaration of Independence, United States.
1787	—	United States Constitution.
1789	—	French Declaration on the Rights of Man and the Citizen, France.
1791	—	United States Bill of Rights.
1864, 1949	—	Geneva Conventions, International Red Cross.
1926	—	Slavery Convention.
1945	—	United Nations Charter, San Francisco.
1947	—	Mohandas Gandhi uses non-violent protests leading India to independence.
1948	—	Universal Declaration of Human Rights (December 10).
1959	—	Declaration on the Rights of Children.
1961	—	Amnesty International founded in London.
1969	—	American Convention on Human Rights.
1989	—	International Convention on the Rights of the Child.
1993	—	United Nation World Conference on Human Rights, Vienna, Austria.
2009	—	Decade of Human Rights Education (1995-2004).

RESOURCE SHEET 3

Preamble of udhr

Whereas recognition of the inherent dignity and of the equal and inalienable rights of all members of the human family is the foundation of freedom, justice and peace in the world,

Whereas disregard and contempt for human rights have resulted in barbarous acts which have outraged the conscience of mankind, and the advent of a world in which human beings shall enjoy freedom of speech and belief and freedom from fear and want has been proclaimed as the highest aspiration of the common people,

Whereas it is essential, if man is not to be compelled to have recourse, as a last resort, to rebellion against tyranny and oppression, that human rights should be protected by the rule of law,

Whereas it is essential to promote the development of friendly relations between nations.

Whereas the peoples of the United Nations have in the Charter reaffirmed their faith in fundamental human rights, in the dignity and worth of the human person and in the equal rights of men and women and have determined to promote social progress and better standards of life in larger freedom, Whereas Member States have pledged themselves to achieve, in co-operation with the United Nations, the promotion of universal respect for and observance of human rights and fundamental freedoms,

Whereas a common understanding of these rights and freedoms is of the greatest importance for the full realization of this pledge,

Now, Therefore the general assembly proclaim this universal declaration of human rights as a common standard of achievement for all peoples and all nations, to the end that every individual and every organ of society, keeping this Declaration constantly in mind, shall strive by teaching and education to promote respect for these rights and freedoms and by progressive measures, national and international, to secure their universal and effective recognition and observance, both among the people of Member States themselves and among the peoples of territories under their jurisdiction.

RESOURCE SHEET 4

Pictures of Human Rights Violence

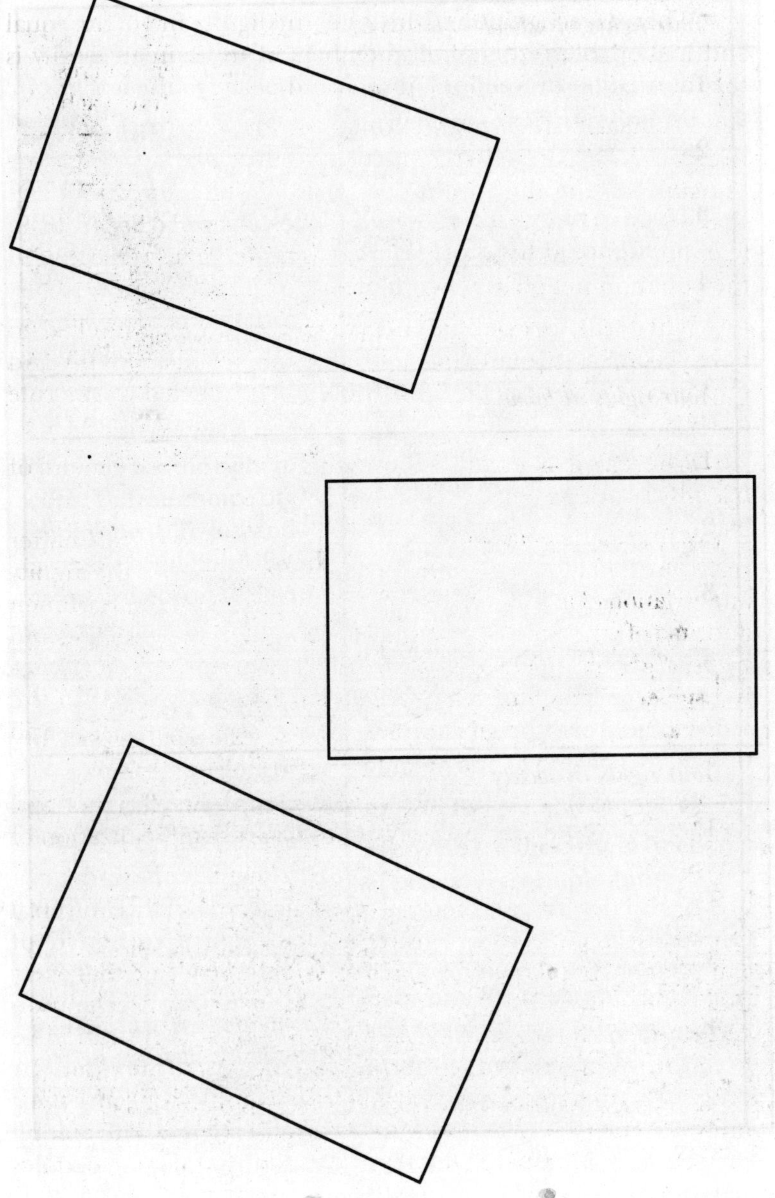

WORKSHEET 2.2

What are your rights in school, home and society

	Your rights in school
	1. 2. 3. 4.
	Your rights at home
	1. 2. 3. 4.
	Your rights in society
	1. 2. 3. 4.

WORKSHEET 2.3

Mention some situations when you feel very happy

Situation one

Situation two

Situation three

Lesson Three

DO YOU KNOW WHAT YOUR RIGHTS ARE?

This lesson provides opportunities to learners to explore what are their rights as a child and as a human being. Student will explore the rights they have and they want. They will also get chance to know how children rights are human rights as well. Lesson will also provide space for learners to understand, why these rights are important for their development.

"I am a child and I do have some rights, why not elders understand this".

What to Do

- What human rights do you have?
- What human rights do we all have?
- Are human rights important?

Will Get Chance to Learn

- Awareness about their human rights.
- Elaborate the concept of rights with reference to all human beings
- Understand and reflect, why rights are important.

What We Need to Facilitate them with

Worksheet 3.1.	—	What rights I have
Resources Sheet 5	—	List of some human rights
Worksheet 3.2	—	List out some human rights other than resource sheet and explain why these are important?
Worksheet 3.3	—	Tick Agree/Disagree

How to Deal with the Class with these Resources

Introduce what we are going to explore today, and distribute the Worksheet 3.1 and provide them time to think and fill the worksheet. Ask them to write, What rights they have? Also ask them? Are these right correct? (in brief)

Distribute the Resource Sheet 5 and ask them to read carefully and match how many rights they have out of the rights written in resource sheet. It will provide chance to explore more rights that learner are not aware.

After that distribute the Worksheet 3.2 and ask them to complete it. But announce that they can not write the same right they have written in worksheet 3.1 and having in resource sheet 5. Let them write some new rights they want, also ask them the reason for choosing those rights.

Ask learners to think and do complete Worksheet 3.3, where they have to tick on Agree or Disagree.

Finally teacher may or may not conclude the class. Depends on the learners understanding during the class.

WORKSHEET 3.1

What are your rights?

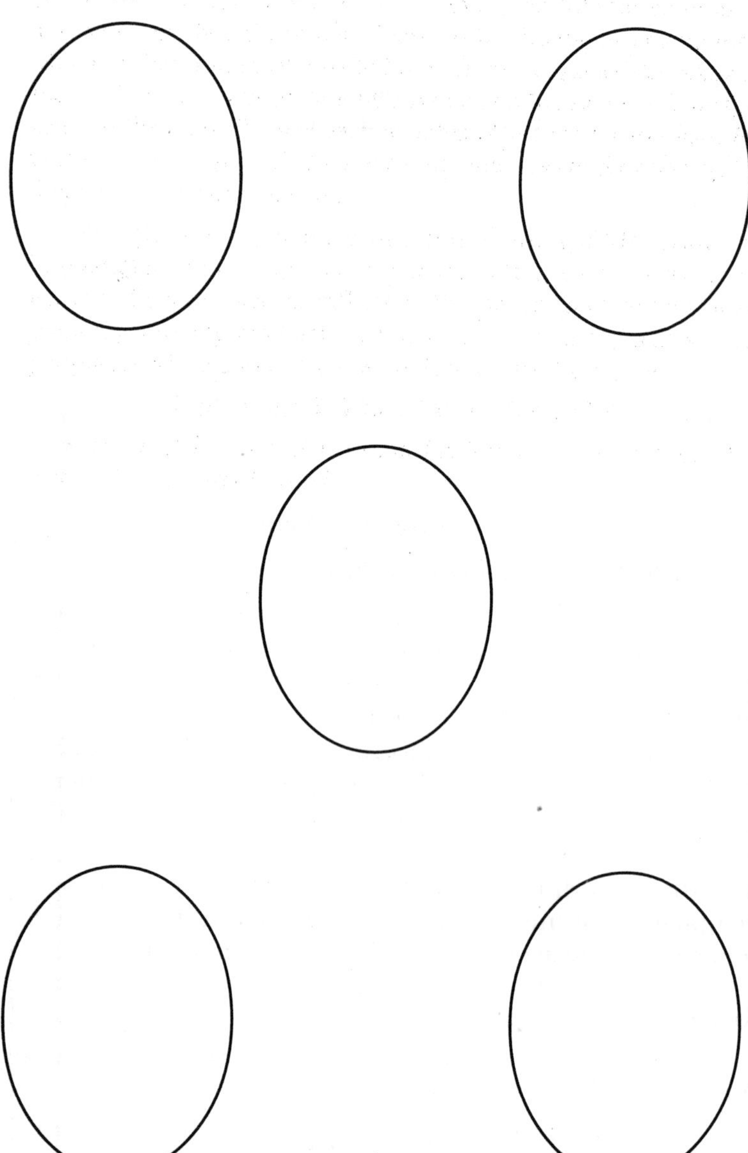

RESOURCE SHEET 5

List of some Human Rights

Right to Education

Right to Live

Right to Speech

Right to Equality

Right to Vote

Right to Food

Right to Marry and have family

Rights against Racism

Right to take part in the Cultural Life of the Community

Right against any kind of Discrimination

Right to be treated like a Human

WORKSHEET 3.2

List our some human rights other than given in Resource Sheet 5 and explain why you consider them important.

Rights you want	Why these are important

WORKSHEET 3.3

Tick Agree/Disagree

As a child I have right to be educated.	(Agree/Disagree)
My aunty is very old. Her son sends her in an old age home. He said she will be happier there. What you say.	(Agree/Disagree)
Mohan getting too much homework every day is no violence of human rights of a child.	(Agree/Disagree)
We all should have right to food.	(Agree/Disagree)
Right to Education is only important from the age 6 to 12.	(Agree/Disagree)
Rishabh classmates tease him as he is very poor.	(Agree/Disagree)
Women has now right to work out. They should work at home and should look after home and children.	(Agree/Disagree)
I am a child I can do mistake.	(Agree/Disagree)

Lesson Four

HUMAN RIGHTS IN INDIA

This lesson provides the understanding about the rights Indian Constitution talk about. Lesson will provide them opportunities to understand the relationship or commonality between Fundamental Rights given by Indian Constitution and UDHR. Lesson also has space to present views about Human Rights Confidently. Lesson will facilitate them to elaborate the rights (fundamental and others) they have.

"Having right is also our Right"

What to Do

- What Rights our constitutional preamble provide us?
- Fundamental Rights and Universal Declaration of Human Rights
- Read, think and speak

Will Get Chance to Learn

- Analyze the preamble of Indian Constitution with respect to rights.
- Compare the Fundamental Rights with Universal Declaration of Human Rights.
- Presentation in an articulated manner.

What We Need to Facilitate them with

Resource Sheet 6	—	Preamble of Indian Constitution
Resource Sheet 7	—	List of Rights given in UDHR
Worksheet 4.1	—	Can you compare the Rights of Indian Constitution with selation of UDHR
Resource Sheet 8	—	Comparative understanding of fundamental rights in India and UDHR

How to Deal with the Class with these Resources

The class agenda is to facilitate learner to know about the rights our preamble talks about. So firstly provide them the Resource Sheet 6 and let them read what this Resource Sheet says. Let them discuss in pair or group of three.

After that distribute Resource Sheet 7 and let them read and think about it individually for some time.

When you feel enough time has been given, just ask them to fill Worksheet 4.1 on the basis of Resource Sheets 6 and 7. It is a very analytical task so provide good enough time to complete it.

For their better understanding about the Rights we have in India and what UDHR says. Provide them Resource Sheet 8 and let them read it thoroughly.

Finely constitute groups of three learners and ask them to prepare bulletin. It may consist at least three information related to human rights. It will help them in many areas like critical thinking, analytical thinking and how to present effectively. Then ask them to present their bulletin one by one.

RESOURCE SHEET 6

PREAMBLE OF INDIAN CONSTITUTION

WE, THE PEOPLE OF INDIA, having solemnly resolved to constitute India into a SOVEREIGN SOCIALIST SECULAR DEMOCRATIC REPUBLIC and to secure to all its citizens:

JUSTICE, social, economic and political;

LIBERTY of thought, expression, belief, faith and worship;

EQUALITY of status and of opportunity; and to promote among them all;

FRATERNITY assuring the dignity of the individual and the unity and integrity of the Nation;

IN OUR CONSTITUENT ASSEMBLY this twenty-sixth day of November, 1949, do HEREBY ADOPT, ENACT AND GIVE TO OURSELVES THIS CONSTITUTION.

RESOURCE SHEET 7

Article 1 Right to Equality

Article 2 Freedom from Discrimination

Article 3 Right to Life, Liberty, Personal Security

Article 4 Freedom from Slavery

Article 5 Freedom from Torture and Degrading Treatment

Article 6 Right to Recognition as a Person before the Law

Article 7 Right to Equality before the Law

Article 8 Right to Remedy by Competent Tribunal

Article 9 Freedom from Arbitrary Arrest and Exile

Article 10 Right to Fair Public Hearing

Article 11 Right to be Considered Innocent until Proven Guilty

Article 12 Freedom from Interference with Privacy, Family, Home and Correspondence

Article 13 Right to Free Movement in and out of the Country

Article 14 Right to Asylum in other Countries from Persecution

Article 15 Right to a Nationality and the Freedom to Change It

Article 16 Right to Marriage and Family

Article 17 Right to Own Property

Article 18 Freedom of Belief and Religion

Article 19 Freedom of Opinion and Information

Article 20 Right of Peaceful Assembly and Association

Article 21 Right to Participate in Government and in Free Elections

Article 22 Right to Social Security

Article 23 Right to Desirable Work and to Join Trade Unions

Article 24 Right to Rest and Leisure

Article 25	Right to Adequate Living Standard
Article 26	Right to Education
Article 27	Right to Participate in the Cultural Life of Community
Article 28	Right to a Social Order that Articulates this Document
Article 29	Community Duties Essential to Free and Full Development
Article 30	Freedom from State or Personal Interference in the above Rights

WORKSHEET 4.1

Can you find out which rights Preamble of Indian Constitution has with relation to Universal Declaration of Human Rights. Also list out rights those have not been included in the Preamble of Indian Constitution. (Refer Resource Sheet 5 and 6).

What is common		What is left to include from UDHR
Preamble of Indian Constitution	*Universal Declaration of Human Rights*	

RESOURCE SHEET 8

Comparative understanding of fundamental rights in India and UDHR.

Fundamental Rights in Indian Constitution	Universal Declaration of Human Rights
Art. 14: The state shall not deny to any person equality before the law or the equal protection of the laws within the territory of India.	*Art:* All are equal before the law and are entitled without any discrimination in violation of this decl- laration and against any incitement incitement to such discrimination.
Equality and Protection of Law	
All are equal before the law and are entitled without any discrimination to equal protection of the law. All are entitled to equal protection against any discrimination in violation of this Declaration and against any incitement to such discrimination.	
Art : 15(1) The state shall not have discrimination against any citizen on the grounds only of religion, race, caste, sex, place of birth or any of them.	*Art. 2:* Everyone is entitled to all the rights and freedoms set forth in this declaration, with our distin-ction of any kind, such as race, colour, sex, language, religion, political or other opinion, national or social origin, property, birth or other status.

(Contd...)

	Art 7 Sentence 2: *(Equality before law)*. All are entitled to equal protection against any discrimination in violation of this declaration and against any incitement to such discrimination.
Art 16 (1): There shall be equality of opportunity for all citizens in the matters relating to employment to any office under the state.	*Art 21 (2):* Everyone has a right to equal access to public service in his country.
Right to Work	
Everyone has the right to work. To free choice of employment. To just and favorable conditions of work and to protection against unemployment.	
Art. 19 (1): All citizens have the — Right to freedom of speech and expression. — Right to assemble peacfully and without arms. — Right to move freely throughout the territory of India. — Right to reside and settle in any part of Indian territory.	*Art. 19:* Everyone has right to freedom of opinion and expression. *Art. 20 (1):* Everyone has the right to freedom of peaceful assembly and association. *Art. 23 (4):* Everyone has the right to form and to join trade unions for the protection of his rights.

(Contd...)

Fundamental Rights in Indian Constitution	Universal Declaration of Human Rights
	Art. 13 (1): Everyone has the right to freedom of movement and residence within the borders of each state.
Right to Expression	
Every one has the right to freedom of opinion and expression; this right includes freedom to hold opinion without interference and to seek, receive and impart information and ideas through any media regardless of frontiers. (Art 19)	
Art. 20 (1) No person shall be convicted of any offence except for a violation of law in force at the time of commission of the act charged as an offence, nor be subjected to a penalty greater than thus which might have been inflicted under the law in force at the time of the commission of the offence.	*Art . 12 (2)* No one shall be held guilty of any penal offence on account to any act or commission which did not constitute a penal offence, under national or international law, at the time when it was committed. Nor shall a heavier penalty be imposed than the one that was applicable at the time the penal offence was committed.
Art. 21: No person shall be deprived of his life or personal liberty except according to procedure established by law.	*Art. 3:* Everyone has the right to life, liberty and security of person. *Art. 9:* No one shall be subjected to arbitrary arrest, detention or exile.

(Contd...)

Right to Life	
Art. 23 (1) Traffic in human being and beggar and other similar forms of forced labor are prohibited and any contravention of this provision shall be an offence punishable in accordance with law.	*Art. 4:* No one shall be held in slavery or servitude and the slave trade shall be prohibited in all forms.
Art. 25(1) Subject to public order, morality and health and to the provisions of this part, all persons are equally entitled to freedom of conscience and right freely to profess, practice and propagate religion.	*Art .18:* Everyone has the right to freedom of thought, conscience and religion; this right includes freedom of change his religion of belief, and freedom, either alone or in community with others and in public or private to manifest his religion or belief in teaching, practice, worship and observation.
Right to Religion	
Everyone has the right to freedom of thought, conscience and religion; this right includes free dom to change his religion or belief, and freedom, either alone or in community with other and in pubic or private, to manifest his religion or belief in teaching, practice, worship and observance (Art 18).	

Lesson Five

RIGHTS FOR ALL

This lesson will facilitate to understand that we all are equal and should be treated equally, whether we are children, women, men, special need children, Minorities etc. Lesson will help to develop a sense of knowing and respecting everyone's rights.

"Are we also human beings?
Then, where are our rights?

What to Do

- What are your rights as children?
- Do women have same rights as men?
- Am I not like others?

Will Get Chance to Learn

- Awareness about children's rights.
- Understand the notion of equality between men and women.
- Know and feel the discrimination exists within society for different people.

What We Need to Facilitate them with

Worksheet 5.1 — What rights you have?

Worksheet 5.2 — Can you write some difference in treatment between men and women?

Worksheet 5.3 — Can you think about the rights of these people?

How to Deal with Class with these Resources

Start class with introducing that we will try to understand our rights.

Distribute Worksheet 5.1 to learners and ask them to sit in pair and fill the worksheet. They will be writing what rights they have at home, school, class, society etc., also ask them to say what right they want.

After completion of this task distribute Worksheet 5.2. They will be exploring the discrimination women have to face at many places. Try to make pair in such a way so that each pair has one girl and one boy.

After that provide them Worksheet 5.3 and ask them to think what right special need people and minorities should have. Teacher need to facilitate them what is special need people and minorities are.

WORKSHEET 5.1

What rights you have?

Place	Rights you have
Home	1. 2. 3.
School	1. 2. 3.
Class	1. 2. 3.
Society	1. 2. 3.
Others	1. 2. 3.

WORKSHEET 5.2

Can you write some difference in treatment between men and women?

Place	Differences
Home	Men
	Women
School	Men
	Women
Class	Men
	Women
Society	Men
	Women
Others	Men
	Women

WORKSHEET 5.3

Can you think about rights of these people?

	Rights
People with differently able	
Minorities	

Lesson Six

DO YOU KNOW WHAT YOURS AND OTHERS RESPONSIBILITIES ARE?

This lesson deals with the notion that human rights can not sustain alone, it is important in the sense that responsibility also should move with it. This lesson will help to facilitate learner to understand some agencies who protect the human rights. In short, what are our responsibilities and what are government responsibilities to project human rights. Because it is a certain believe that right and responsibilities work together.

"My rights are your responsibilities and your rights are my responsibilities"

What to Do

- Who protect our human rights?
- How can you make sure that your and others human rights are protected.

Will Get Chance to Learn

- Understand different agencies that protect our human rights.
- Develop a sense of responsibility to respect towards ones own and others rights.
- Explore the possibilities regarding, how to protect our human rights.

What We Need to Facilitate them with

Resource Sheet cum Worksheet 1	—	Some agencies who protect our rights
Worksheet 6.1	—	Respect, protect and promote human rights
Worksheet 6.2	—	Do think and talk

How to Deal with the Class with these Resources

Distribute Resource Sheet cum Worksheet 1 to the learners. Ask them to read and then fill in groups. Group may be of four learners. Teacher also needs to facilitate them in task in form of scaffolding and prompting.

Worksheet 6.1 will help learners to think about how they can Respect, Protect and Promote human rights at different level. Let them do this work in groups. Provide facilitation wherever you feel class need it.

After this provide them Worksheet 6.2 and ask to discuss the given situations in their group. Some associated questions has also been given with the situation. Ask them to think and talk over them.

WORKSHEET CUM RESOURCE SHEET1

Some agencies who protect human rights

Constitution

Police

Judiciary

Non-governmental organizations

Can you think of some other agencies like home etc. who protect Human Rights?

WORKSHEET 6.1

Respect, Protect and Promote Human Rights

How can you respect, protect and promote Human Rights?

Personal level	Respect
	Protect
	Promote
School level	Respect
	Protect
	Promote
Community level	Respect
	Protect
	Promote
National level	Respect
	Protect
	Promote
Global level	Respect
	Protect
	Promote

WORKSHEET 6.2

Do think and talk

Every one has right to express their views freely and their views must be listened.

Share some situation when this right is being denied. What you think you can do in such situations?

One person is not allowed to enter in temple because of some reason.

Can you think in your group what may be the reason; also discuss some other event like this if you have observed from your everyday life.

Parents bought a good expensive doll for their daughter and one foot ball for their son.

Can you trace any kind of discrimination in this? What is that? Discuss some other discrimination like this you have observed.

In my family most of the time my father takes all the important decision as he is the earner in my family.

Discuss the situation in your group. What are the different views about this situation?

Lesson Seven

ARE WE ALL DIFFERENT OR SOMETHING IS COMMON?

This lesson specifically will talk about the problems and benefits of diversities in a country like India. It will also help to develop a positive attitude towards solving such issues. Lesson will provide space to learn how to respect others perspective irrespective of anything. Lesson will facilitate to develop an understanding about common values.

"Some says we are unite but some says we are individually different, how to know about it"

What to Do

- Can you think in what ways you are different from others?
- Can you think what commonalities you have with others?
- What are the common values for all?

Will Get Chance to learn

- Understand the notion of diversity.
- Explore the notions of possibilities for unity in diversity.
- Develop a sense of consciences.

What We Need to Facilitate them with

Worksheet 7.1	—	what common we have?
Worksheet 7.2	—	are we different from each others?
Resource Sheet 9	—	Value cards
Worksheet 7.3	—	Can we make conscience?

How to Deal with the Class with these Resources

As mentioned above, this lesson will help learner to understand the concept of diversity and unity. Provide them Worksheet 7.1 and ask them to sit in group and discuss and write, What kind of commonalities they have?

Now distribute Worksheet 7.2 the same way as Worksheet 6.1 was also done and ask them to discuss and write the discussion.

After that distribute the Resource Sheet 9 to the learners and ask them to read the Resource Sheet in group. Provide enough time to them to understand the concepts mentioned on the sheet.

Finally provide them the Worksheet 7.3 and help them to come on some consciences about rights and values those they feel are mandatory to all human beings. Also ask them to write, Why they feel so?

Teacher may conclude the class or may leave it open ended.

WORKSHEET 7.1

What common we have?

Talk with your pair and write what are the commonalities you have (in terms of opinion about something, and all)

	Commonalities
1.	
2.	
3.	
4.	
5.	

WORKSHEET 7.2

What ways we are different?

Write some differences you have from you pair (in terms of opinion about something, and all)

	Differences
1.	
2.	
3.	
4.	
5.	

RESOURCE SHEET 9

Peace

Resolving conflict without violence

Fairness

Treating people fairly

Equality

People should be treated equally not matter who they are

Freedom

Freedom for individuals to be who they want to be, freedom of speech.

Tolerance

Accepting and valuing people's differences.

Respect of others

Respecting other people's views and way of life.

WORKSHEET 7.3

Can we make conscience

On the basis of Worksheets 6.1, 6.2 and Resource Sheet 9, can you think of some common values those are universal and why?

Values	Why you chose this value

Lesson Eight

WHERE ARE THE PROBLEMS AND POSSIBILITIES?

This lesson will deal with some important issues related to human rights. It will provide space to share learner's ideas and experiences with respect of human rights violation. They will also get chance to relate their own role in promotion of these rights. Will also get chance to reflect, are they doing something wrong with respect to human rights? Lesson also has space to realize them how people can do wrong to others even they do bother and think they are doing wrong.

"Don't you think, problems itself carry the solutions"

What to Do

- Why we do wrong to others?
- Any experience where you feel you did wrong to someone. Did you realize and feel uncomfortable later?
- What we should do, if we do wrong to some one?

Will Get Chance to Learn

- Analyse situations critically
- Reflect upon their past experiences
- Think analytically for solutions

What We Need to Facilitate them with

Worksheet 8.1 — What wrong generally we do to others?

Worksheet 8.2 — Share your one experience.

Worksheet 8.3 — Suggest something, what you do when you will do wrong to someone.

How to Deal with the Class with these Resources

You may start your class with a good story which consist of violation of human rights.

Provide Worksheet 8.1 to learners to explore their general views that what they think generally what wrong people to do with each other, it may be in terms of class, family, society, playground, anywhere.

In Worksheet 8.2 ask them to write one experience where they feel they had done wrong and after that how they felt. If some says they had not done anything like this, then ask such students to think "if" they do, then what they will feel.

Worksheet 8.3 will facilitate them to think analytical as this worksheet demands some suggestions after doing something wrong to some one. Learners must be sharing different experiences. Also help them to respect each other views and suggestions.

WORKSHEET 8.1

What wrong generally we do with others?

Write generally what you think people do wrong with each other. Like they do not respect etc.

	Wrong we do with others generally
1.	
2.	
3.	
4.	
5.	
6.	
7.	
8.	

WORKSHEET 8.2

Share your one experience

Write your any one experience where you feel you had done wrong to some one. How you come to know that you did wrong and then what you did?

WORKSHEET 8.3

Suggest something what you do to resolve the problem when you will do wrong to someone.

	Suggestions
1.	
2.	
3.	
4.	
5.	
6.	
7.	
8.	

Lesson Nine

RETHINKING ABOUT RIGHTS

This lesson will provide space for learner to show and use their creativity on the basis of whatsoever they have explored about human rights till now. They will talk about what are other areas and field in which they want to know human rights. The area of interest may be anything. It will be very useful lesson for both (teacher and learners). They will be exploring new areas within human rights which they want to explore.

"Are Human Rights only those, what we have learned or I can think beyond"

What to Do

- What else except this course you want to learn and understand about human rights.

Will Get Chance to Learn

- Analyse critically and reflectively the entire course they have gone through.

What We Need to Facilitate them with

Worksheet 9.1—Develop your course of human rights.

How to Deal with the Class with these Resources

This activity is very important for the development of learners' analytical, critical and reflective thinking. Let them sit in group of 4 or 5 and discuss and develop their course of human rights. Ensure that they should not repeat every thing from existing course, except some areas which they feel they can take. Ask them to write, Why they want to take that component in their course?

After this exercise display all course developed by leaner on display board, so that all can read each others and can discuss.

WORKSHEET 9.1

Develop your course of Human Rights

	What to include	Why to include
1.		
2.		
3.		
4.		
5.		
6.		
7.		
8.		

5

How to Include Human Rights in Pedagogy

Pervious chapter dealt with the teaching of human rights as we believe that only including human rights perspective in pedagogy will not be able to facilitate the entire process of teaching and learning. This lesson will provide scope to explore and understand that how we can make our classroom pedagogy human rights perspective-based pedagogy

Pedagogy refers to a planned learning process through which learners develop cognitively, experientially and affectively in response to interaction with facilitators of learning. Such planned interaction between learning facilitators and learners must pursue an explicit purpose, which in the case of human rights education, is awareness of and capacity to act to further human rights aspirations.

Human rights norms themselves, in particular the Universal Declaration, the International Covenant on Economic, Social and Cultural Rights, the Convention on the Rights of the Child and the Vienna Declaration and Plan of Action, define the objective of all education as the full development of the human personality and potential. This objective can best be attained by enabling learners creatively and analytically to construct knowledge and be able to deconstruct fallacious or distorted knowledge concerning their own situation in society and history and reconstructing that knowledge by using critical, reflective, and moral faculties which it is the facilitator's task to assist them in acquiring. Education thus understood is a life-long process in which individuals become at different times and to differing degrees both facilitators of learning and learners. It is, therefore, essential, although frequently neglected, that the learning processes respect the historical, social, psychological, ethnic, gender, linguistic and other contexts of the learners.

Now, let understand what specifically need to be included in pedagogy so that it can become more human rights perspective based.

Negotiated and Agreed Classroom Code and Conduct between Teacher and Students

It is a fact that if we are providing space to students to speak and negotiate on different ideas then they will learn better. So providing space to negotiation to learners is very important. How they will talk and behave with each other and teacher should be determined after discussion between students and teacher. Same we can do with teaching learning processes. Developing such code of conducts will also facilitate the teaching learning processes. In many ways negotiated teaching learning process provide better space for learning:

- Negotiation is a mean for responsible membership of the class-room community.
- Negotiation can construct and reflect learning as an emancipated process.
- Negotiation can activate the social and cultural resources of classroom processes.
- Negotiation enables learners to exercise their active agency in learning.
- Negotiation can inform or extend teachers to pedagogic strategies.

In such a way their will be respect of dignity of both teacher as well as students. So using negotiation with learners with reference to class and how they want to learn incorporate human rights perspective.

Criteria of Regular Feedback to the Teacher by the Learners

Generally in school we observe and being observed in data analysis that there is teacher oriented class. There is not space for students feedback to teacher. It seems to be one way process. What teacher says and does is ultimate in class. In such a situation we can not expect students to understand concept effectively. Effective feedback always facilitate learner and teacher also. And is a very humanistic approach to reach to the learner understanding. With this, teacher can also know in what areas he/she need some development. But it is very important that teacher should take that feedback very positively instead partially. Such an environment will come under human right perspective.

Depending on the students and their grade level, this sort of behavior might give higher results. We might want to consider periodically being more direct in our questions for feedback. For example, at the end of class or after a project, we could ask our students to fill out a questionnaire with pointed questions: "How much time did I spend helping you this last week? How many questions did I ask you? Do you feel I successfully encouraged you to do your best? What did you like about the learning activity? What do you want to see more of? What do you want to see less of?"

Now, if we are smart, we will do some of our own evaluation and reflection to prepare us for the answers we are likely to receive from our students. We want to look especially at the correlation of what we say we believe about students and learning and how we are applying that belief in our instruction. For example, if we believe that all students can learn, how are we making sure that this happens? This understanding itself is full of human rights perspective.

Ultimately, in order to create a high-performance learning team in our classrooms, the students and the teacher have to be accountable to one another. The trust created in such an environment will allow us to ask and answer the hard questions— "How am I doing as your teacher?" and "How am I doing as your student?" I am interested in hearing your thoughts, and some of the answers your students have given to your hard questions.

Such environment will help to create classroom a human rights based classroom.

Full Participation of Learners in their Teaching Learning Processes Respectfully

While increasing participation is an obvious goal in courses that include frequent discussions and small-group work, it is also important in a class course. In short, if only a few students participate by volunteering answers, asking questions, or contributing to discussions, class sessions become to some extent a lost opportunity to assess and promote learning. You can improve student participation in your class by devoting time and thought to shaping the environment and planning each class session. Furthermore, the way in which you interact, both verbally and non-verbally, communicates to students your attitude about participation. This will make your class human right perspective based class.

Ideally, the goal of increasing participation is not to have every student participate in the same way or at the same rate. Instead, it is to create an environment in which all participants have the opportunity to learn and in which the class explores issues and ideas in depth, from a variety of viewpoints. Some students will raise their voices more than others; this variation is a result of differences in learning styles as well as differences in personalities. For example, some students who do not speak often in class are *reflective learners*, who typically develop ideas and questions in their minds before speaking; others are shy students who feel uncomfortable speaking in front of groups (at least initially). Many students who frequently volunteer to contribute are *active learners*, who typically think while they speak. The instructor's goal is to create conditions that enable students of various learning styles and personalities to contribute. To reach this goal, you will need to take extra steps to encourage quiet students to speak up and, occasionally, ask the more verbose students to hold back from commenting in order to give others a chance.

The whole above thing should be done while respecting learners dignity. Dealing with students with full respect in classroom will encourage them to participate more effectively in teaching learning process. It is their right to participate in learning. They are not passive receivers. They can construct knowledge and can develop their own ways of leaning. So it is very important to make your class learner centered if you want to make your class more human rights perspective based.

Students Fully Involved in the Evaluation of their own Learning

It is not enough only to involve learners in their learning process. It is also very important to involve them in their evaluation process, so they can feel some authority on their learning.

While teacher-made tests and standardized tests give us information about student learning, they do not provide all the information. Alternate forms of assessment can generate that other information. Self-evaluation is defined as students evaluating the quality of their work, based on evidence and explicit criteria, for the purpose of doing better work in the future. When we teach students how to assess their own progress, and when they do so against known and challenging quality standards, we find that there is a lot to gain. They also develop the sense of responsibility and initiation. And these are children's rights. Self-evaluation is a potentially powerful technique because of its impact on student performance through enhanced self-efficacy and increased intrinsic motivation.

Doing this will also make them more disciplined and hardworking without any extra burdon and work. In such an environment students will be more confident to ask question, in responding to the question and sharing their views and it is a great step towards making them empowered. And if they become empowered through such environment that proves that environment has essence of human rights.

Peer Evaluations

Some time it happened that some students are not evaluating themselve properly, and therefore there will not be fair evaluation which is it self against the human rights perspective. In such a situation peer evaluation is a vary good process for evaluation, which will also delimit the possibilities of unfair evaluation.

Peer evaluation is the evaluation of creative work or performance by other people in the same field in order to maintain or enhance the quality of the work or performance in that field. Peer review helps maintain and enhance quality both directly by detecting weaknesses and errors in specific works and performance and indirectly by providing a basis for making decisions about rewards and punishment that can provide a powerful incentive to achieve excellence.

But before deciding to do peer review, it's essential that you consider your pedagogical reasons for using it. Some time it happens that students are not that expert to evaluation like a trained expert. Rather than see peer review as a substitute for your comments, there is a need to value peer review as a way to get students actively involved in their own learning. By providing opportunities to learns to read their peers' writing and talk together about the process of drafting and revising, it will encourage them to become more self- conscious about their own writing process and to begin and to take control over that process.

Students have Responsibility for aspects of Classroom Organization

Teachers need to provide such environment so that they can feel their responsibilities with respect to class and in general. Daily routine organizational things also should be managed by students such as availability of *chouck* and dusters etc. also appoint rotational *monitors* for the class. Provide responsibilities to the *monitor* and the entire class for class cleanness. (it does not mean that they will clean the class but they may approach to the person who is responsible for cleaning) Providing such responsibilities will develop a sense of concerns with the system of class. Such initiation also facilitate them to develop the confidence to talk about their rights and duties and this is something which we want our students should develop.

Choice of Learning should be given to Learners

Choice in the area of the learning is emphasized ideas of student-centeredness as students might not only choose what to study, but how and why that topic might be an interesting one to study. He also emphasizes Rogers' belief that students' perceptions of the world were important, that they were relevant and appropriate. This definition therefore emphasizes the concept of students having 'choice' in their learning.

Choice of learning does not focus on the teacher transmitting knowledge, from the expert to the novice. In contrast, it describe student-centered learning as focusing on the students' learning and 'what students do to achieve this, rather than what the teacher does'. This idea emphasizes the concept of the student 'doing'.

In short if we want to understand the importance, when choice of learning is with learner are:

1. The reliance on active rather than passive learning.
2. An emphasis on deep learning and understanding.
3. Increased responsibility and accountability on the part of the student.
4. An increased sense of autonomy in the learner.
5. An interdependence between teacher and learner.
6. Mutual respect within the learner teacher relationship.
7. A reflexive approach to the teaching and learning process on the part of both teacher and learner.

So choice of learning needs to be given to learners. In this way they will develop a sense of authority on their on learning, which leads our pedagogy more towards human right perspective.

Mutual Support and Collaboration should be Emphasis

To use human right perspective base in our classes, it is very important that there must be mutual support and collaboration not only between student and teacher, moreover it is required among learners too. Mutual support and collaboration helps them in their learning in more significance manner.

Mutual support plays an very important part of the working culture of any school and classroom system. Now we need to look mutual support as integral part of teaching learning process. It is import because in today's world where every day knowledge keep changing, mutual support and understanding provide an wider perspective to learner to understand the concepts and issues. Therefore, it is important that students learn to function in a team environment so that they will have teamwork skill when they enter the workforce. Also, research tells us that students learn best from tasks that involve doing tasks and social interactions.

Collaborative learning should be included in almost every classroom, but some teachers struggle with having students work cooperatively. There are a number of reasons for this struggle, which include the need to develop good team exercises and the added difficulty in assessing the individual performance of the team members. This is where understanding how to teach effective teamwork becomes a crucial task for the teacher.

Now we can easily think, if we have such an environment in our classes, then we do not need to bother much about human rights perspective as it itself carry human right perspective inherent within the process, where every one is free and ready to understand each others ideas and understanding. This is one of the basic premises of human rights perspective in classroom practices.

Variety of Teaching Strategies Needs to be used with Respect to how Learner can and want to learn (Learner may think differently)

This aspect which I feel is very important. Generally what teacher do they decide one strategy to teach and use that only. (Analysis of classes also proved that.) There is no space where student are being asked how you want to learn about any given topic. Classes are very much teacher dominated in all most all respect. Such an environment develop a kind of alienation in learners from learning. They also start feeling that, this is something that which is forced on them and not their own, which result in bad outcomes of learning.

So it become very important that students should have this much freedom so that they can choose their own way of learning.

It does not mean that there is no role for teacher in class. Their role is to introduce different new strategies to the learner (though learner may develop their own) so that they can decide to own any one of them and can take responsibility of learning. This environment will help in many ways.

- Teacher will become more enthusiastic when his/her students are actively involved.
- Learners will be able to understand the relevance of the material, as they have to decide or choose their learning strategies.
- When learners are organizing the course to decide their learning strategies, it will befit and facilitate their thinking processes and promote it to the higher level.
- In the same regard learner will be able to understand the appropriate difficulty level of the material.
- Active involvement of students.
- Teacher proving some strategies and students are also developing their own strategies, so varieties of strategies and activities will be available for class.

These opportunities will provide confidence in learners. It will also help them to learn how to respect each other's ideas. The basic thing they will learn is to take responsibilities, which is a very higher value we all should be enculturate and we will be able to make our classroom more human rights perspective- based.

Rapport between Teacher and Students

It was also being observed in classroom observation and interviews of teacher that they are least concern about what students think about them. They feel and believe, their only work is to come in class and teach (that also is problematic). But researches show that there is great need for a good rapport between teacher and students. I personally believe, there is a great need that teachers should feel the concern with student, not only for their teaching even in general.

When a teacher shows he/she genuinely cares about a student it tends to set students apart from academic work and helps gain their cooperation, keeping them motivated and on task. Generally, this might be viewed as teachers having positive rapport with students. Essentials of building rapport include harmonic situations and focus on the building of self-esteem in one-self and others by creating a warm, honest, and sincere human relationship. Building a warm, honest, and sincere rapport comes easy with best friends, families, companions and neighbors. Why then is it so challenging to create this type of bond with students?

I believe that learning is the crucial factor, but high school students need to feel welcomed and accepted just as much, if not more, than younger students. By using the first day of class in the high school to bond with students, positive relationships or the building of rapport begins, and thus, the business of learning can begin, because if we really want our pedagogy based on human rights perspective-based we need to understand that content, teaching and learning all are for human being and human beings are not for that. So developing good rapport will certainly facilitate a teacher to facilitate learners in a more progressive manner.

Use of Appropriate, Concrete, and Understandable Examples

It is learners' right that whatsoever is happening in the class, they should understand. If teacher uses some inappropriate situation which does not suite to the content, students can not understand. So to respect their right to know and understand teachers are required to understanding that he/she need to use examples and situations according to situation in way, where there is no humiliation happening with students. Some time it happened that teacher does not bother what examples he/she is using to explain the concept and that influence students negatively. So teacher need to be very sensitive while quoting any example.

Teaching Assistant and Scaffolding should be Provided in terms of Learner's Ability to Learn

Each and every individual is different from each other in one respect to other, as we all belong to different background and so carry a different context. It is the responsibility of a teacher to look after this. He/she should be sensitive enough about these diversities. It is also universally accepted that it is very important and difficult also to include this in teaching learning process. But it is not impossible. As we have discussed in earlier points that developing a good rapport with students helps. So that rapport will facilitate here also and will help teacher to know students background, so that he/she can be more careful while providing any kind of support (scaffolding).

Scaffolding describes specialized teaching strategies geared to support learning when students are first introduced to a new subject. Scaffolding gives students a context, motivation, or foundation from which to understand the new information that will be introduced during the coming lesson.

Scaffolding techniques should be considered fundamental to good, solid teaching for all students, not just for those with learning disabilities or second language learners. In order for learning to progress, scaffolds should be gradually removed as instruction continues, so that students will eventually be able to demonstrate comprehension independently.

There is a possibility in a single classroom where students from all class, caste, religion and region have so assistance provided by teacher or facilitator, also incorporate all this in a healthy way. There will be some students those can learn very fast and quickly but others can not. So it become essential to use different ways of learning in the class as students abilities to learning and understanding are different. It is their right also to get such treatment and environment. Ultimately agenda is to make them independent learner and knowledge constructor. So with all keeping in mind what we have just discussed in above two paragraphs, a teacher need to:

- Define the task at hand for students to complete. Explain what it is through words and/or visual aids (if has).
- Model the specific learning skill. This can be done through direct or indirect instruction.
- Give specifics to students through a sequence of events. Instruct step-by-step.
- Provide students with prompts, cues or hints to assist them in getting to the answer or skill on their own. You are essentially giving them a push in the right direction without giving the answer or skill away.
- Step back from the learning that is taking place to observe students' independent work. Make sure that students are ready to work on their own before you slowly remove yourself. You should see students grasp the concept on their own. During this time you can do some type of formative assessment of students. For example, you could give points for participation or check for understanding.

Respecting Learners' Views

As already being mentioned and discussed that classrooms in a country like India always carry diversity in terms of cast, class, religion and region and because of this there are multiple people in a class with multiple contexts and backgrounds. These different diversities formulate a platform for all of us to think differently. And this is also very obvious that with such a divers situation there will be agreements and disagreements. Now the role of a teacher becomes very crucial in relation to how to deal with the class. In such a situation and otherwise it becomes very important respecting students views is because when they say something, that something carry a lot of context behind it and if teacher think about it nothing can happened better than this. It will facilitate learners to feel that their views are not 'nonsense' and has some 'sense'. What has said above is also important because this is directly concern with the respecting learners' dignity. It also has this underpinning that learners' voice should be highly appreciated.

There is need to be Ensure that Learners' Respect and Value each other's Commonalities and Differences

We all are common and different in some aspects or other. In last some points we discussed that how it is important for teacher to respect students views and ideas. Here I would like to emphasise that learners should respect and values each other's ideas, commonalities and differences are also equally important. Classroom is a community itself and if there will more disparities in terms of working together, doing collaborative works and all, then classroom system will not function properly and will cause for serious implications. So the environment of the class should be free from unwanted conflicts. Class is a place where if teacher wants and has capabilities can facilitate to develop harmony and consciences, so that conflict, those are harmful for society, can be stopped to develop. Only human right perspective-based class can provide such space for learners.

It is also important to keep in mind that the agenda is not to create a culture of silence instead agenda is to create a positive atmosphere so that we can understand each other's point of view with full of positive attitude.

Equal Opportunities to All

Human rights perspective believes that in a class every one should get equal opportunity to participate in all practices taking place in class. What is being observed in classroom observation is that teachers have their favorites in class (generally students those are bright in studies, some time it also happened in terms of caste, region, religion etc.). It is a clear violation of human rights of children. In this situation some of them will not be able to participate and gradually will become marginalized and will also lose interest from studies. To teacher need to be very carefully that every one is getting equal opportunity to participate.

Here I would like to add that equal does not mean equal to all. There are specific or special needs people in each class and certainly they need especial attention and facilities. The notion of equal opportunities to all include this perspective as well.

So including this understanding in teaching-learning processes will promote human right perspective.

Need to be Concern

What we mean by concern? I will say when my daughter is not well, I will take leave from my office whether how much important task I have to leave. I will do it because I am concerned with my daughter. And if my boss will say no, you can not go, even then I will go, and I will do whatsoever I can do. So, that shows the concern. Now question to think. Do you have concern with your students? Are you ready to do everything for them? Do we feel their problems? Do you understand what they want to say to us? Do we genuinely have concern why students are dropping out and why they are getting fail? Certainly not. And if yes, what we did for them? These are certain question which we all need to ask ourselves and to work positively in this regard if we want a human rights based class. It will come if we will feel concern with school, with class, and above all with our students considering them human being.

Being Reflective and Promoting Reflection

Reflection is the process which can take place at three level—reflection before action, reflection in action and reflection after action. Now let see how reflection will facilitate the human rights perspective-based class. Reflection is thinking for an extended period by linking recent experiences to earlier ones in order to promote a more complex and inter-related mental schema. The thinking involves looking for commonalities, differences, and inter-relations beyond their superficial elements. The goal is to develop higher order thinking skill and directly linked with metacognitive abilities. So as a teacher we need to do certain things to be reflective and also facilitate our learners to be reflective. First let see what a teacher need to understand.

1. Teachers should learn to frame and reframe complex or ambiguous problems, test out various interpretations, and then modify actions consequently.

2. They should try to extend and systematize their thoughts by looking back upon their actions, some time after they have taken place.
3. They need to understand certain activities labeled as reflective, such as the use of journals or group discussions following practical experiences, are helpful to put them on path of reflection.
4. They should consciously account for the wider historic, cultural, and political values or beliefs in framing practical problems to arrive at a solution.

In short if I will say, if a teacher think what is going to do in class today (before action), what all I am doing in class (on action) and what all I did today in my class (after action) he is on path of reflection. Now, if a teacher is doing this then next responsibility is to facilitate learners to starts thinking reflectively and if we teachers succeed students will be able to

- examine their own learning process.
- take responsibility for their own learning.
- see "gaps" in their learning.
- determine strategies that supported their learning.
- celebrate risk taking and inquiry.
- set goals for future experiences.
- see changes and development over time.

Thus, if teacher and students are doing reflection-based learning then human right perspective will always exist there.

Learning as a Process, not a Product

We generally consider learning as a outcome or end product. But if we talk about human rights perspective we will be talking of learning a process. When w talk about learning as a product, everything starts and finishes at the product, and if we see this approach in classroom teaching, ultimate agenda is getting good marks in exam. Where-as the other view, which consider learning a process, is more liberal and believe that nothing is absolute and reality is subjective because the knowing process of that reality is also subjective. So this view more focus on learning a process not a product. Believing in first idea has some problem as ultimate thing is product (result), teacher will deal with students in a single way, the way through which they will get good marks. But the other view will consider the individual process understanding and learning and accordingly will deal with the students. In such process more focus will be on providing opportunities but not only one mean to learn an produce. So from human right perspective more goes with the second view where learning as a product is being more emphasized.

We have discussed above many ways in which we can promote human rights perspective in pedagogy. If we will be able to do that we will be moving towards a 'Culture of Human Rights' in Pedagogy. It will propose a pedagogy of transformation in light of the reality that the magnitude of human rights violations as well as the obstacles to change are so vast that what is required goes beyond the need for amelioration and reform. Such a pedagogy is to be contrasted with a pedagogy of social reproduction in which patterns of hierarchy, abuse and exclusion may be legitimized and preserved.

Formal education (schools, universities, vocational and technical schools, professional schools, etc.) and other learning environments can be and sometimes are places where faculty, students and staff have the opportunity to search for meaning, to pursue the search for justice and to develop their unique beings in an atmosphere of safety, caring, and compassion. We strongly believe that students who are fully engaged in such an educational process are much more likely to challenge social and cultural domination. Vested interests, persistent habits, and bureaucratic attitude can be obstacles to the incorporation of a human rights pedagogy into formal education.

The pedagogy required for such a process will undoubtedly involve a wide variety of methods and approaches that should reflect and be guided by the principles that are basic to in the human rights pedagogy. These principles include:

- Full respect for all people regardless of class, caste, sexual preference, race, gender, religion, income, ability, age, or other conditions.
- Participation of students in their own education and sharing in the decision-making process.
- The celebration of human experience as an expression of diversity and uniqueness as well as an important source of knowledge and wisdom.
- The vital importance of social responsibility.

In this connection, it is important to reaffirm the rights and responsibilities of individual teachers to participate in professional decisions on such matters as the development of curriculum materials and instructional approaches. In addition, teachers have the responsibility to relate to students in a manner consistent with human rights principles. Valuable guidance regarding the human rights that must be respected in teacher-pupil relations may be found in the International Convention on the Rights of the Child, which includes the child's rights to dignity, security, participation, identity, freedom of thought, access to information, and privacy. Full respect for these rights would transform most learning environments and foster human rights education.

The content of human rights education necessarily varies with the learning environment. Among the elements that are frequently pertinent are the following:

- The historical development of human rights and a critical understanding of the history of the struggle for human rights with particular emphasis on successful models;
- The use and abuse of international and national forces;
- The nature and extent of human rights violations,—locally, regionally, nationally, as well as in the schools;
- The international instruments protecting human rights such as
    - The Universal Declaration of Human Rights,
    - The International Covenants on Human Rights,

- The Convention on the Rights of the Child,
- The Convention on the Elimination of all forms of Discrimination against Women,
- The agencies and institutions of remediation,
- The critical understanding of related concepts such as justice, freedom, democracy and peace and the experiences with the realities of human rights concerns of students and others.

The UN definition correctly states that "human rights education should involve more than the provision of information and should constitute a comprehensive life-long process by which people at all levels in development and in all strata of society learn respect for the dignity of others and the means and methods of ensuring that respect in all societies". This definition implies knowledge of remedies provided in the national and international legal and political institutions as well as forms of action when those institutions fail to provide such remedies.

In addition to appropriate knowledge and understanding, human rights education operating within a context of the affirmation of the value of human life and dignity, involves developing the capacity to care and be compassionate; to commit to the struggle for human rights and to understanding the role of non-violent civil disobedience has played in this struggle; to exercise personal responsibility and human agency; to develop the imagination and creativity necessary to envision and create a just and caring community; to develop the critical consciousness necessary to sustain rational judgment; the skills of self-reflection and personal transformation; the courage and strength necessary to sustain the struggle.

With respect to popular education and out-of-school youth, pedagogies of transformation derived from popular struggle are an important ingredient in human rights education. As we seek to bring human rights education to the world's youth, we are all mindful that such education must honor their experiences, reflect their concerns and be relevant to youth culture. The great numbers of the world's youth to whom formal schooling is not available should have the opportunity to engage in human rights education in other learning environments.

Regarding teacher education teachers, facilitators, organizers and trainers should demonstrate, in their personal behaviours and teaching methods, respect for the dignity of learners with varying capacities. Those who initiate and guide learning processes based upon a pedagogy of transformation will require capacities to face a range of challenges imposed by the democratization of the teaching/learning process. Thus, we see the need for major and radical changes in the preparation of teachers and facilitators and those who are responsible for coordinating human rights education.

Where women are excluded from formal education and production of knowledge, human rights education require a two-fold strategy: first, women and girls should be allowed equal access to formal education, including affirmative modes of overcoming traditional patterns of exclusion. Second, special opportunities should be encouraged to develop alternative modes of learning and specific forms of women's human rights education, recognizing women's production of knowledge. In addition, human rights education should encourage positive action to achieve equality and representation of women in society and professions, particularly to increase their access to positions of power and responsibility in the fields traditionally dominated by men. Such measures should prevail until substantial equality in sharing of power and influence is achieved.

Universities often open extraordinary opportunities for social mobility. They also train elites to join the power structure in government and business by imparting privileged knowledge and imbedding networks of collaboration that reinforce structures of domination. At the same time, universities that respect academic freedom and promote independent research are critically important places where alternative modes of analysis, theorizing, and action can be developed. Universities are, therefore, valuable locations for developing pedagogies of human rights education and training students to engage in professional human rights work. One of the tasks of human rights education is to expand these opportunities.

Vocational and technical education offer a special occasion to develop pedagogies that relate to the skills of the workplace which students are attending. Such institutions acquire in the role of workers in the political economy and the human rights struggles that context. Similarly, professional schools require specific pedagogies aimed at engaging future lawyers, health and medical professionals, journalists, architects, administrators, military personnel and others in a reflection on the human rights dimensions of their professional field and on the application of their professional skills to the tasks of the human rights struggle.

The relations between school and community are vital dimensions of human rights education directed towards the transformation of societies. The schools and all learning agents and sites should have close and integrated relationships with their respective communities.

6

Learning Environment and Innovative Methodologies

In order to achieve the human rights perspective-based pedagogy described in previous chapter, educators and other facilitators of learning need to develop and use innovative methodologies adapted to a wide range of learning environments. By learning environments, we understand all places where people interact in a way in which there is a potential for learning through exchange, sharing of ideas, reception of information, contact and communication. We may consider these as synergistic communities, i.e., where the more interaction occurs, the more viable it becomes. These places and spaces may be institutionalized for the explicit and permanent purpose of education (formal), or for other purposes and used incidentally or provisionally for education (informal), or not institutionalized at all (non-formal). These environments may also be the occurrence of a spontaneous event. The potential of these sites is variable, based on culture, socio-economic conditions, etc. These sites may even come into conflict and contradiction. The following is a suggested and open list of learning environments where specific pedagogies for human rights education have been or might be developed.

No matter what the setting—whether a classroom, a senior citizens' center, or a religious organization—common principles inform the methods used to teach human rights. These principles should be communicated through every aspect of good human rights perspective-based pedagogy: Provide open minded examination of human rights concerns with opportunities for participants to arrive at positions different from those of the facilitator. Include an international dimension to the human rights theme being examined (e.g. how it manifests itself both at home and abroad). Avoid too much focus on human rights abuses. Emphasize human rights as a positive value system and a standard to which everyone is entitled. Affirm the belief that the individual can make a difference and provide examples of individuals who have done so. Include an action dimension that provides participants with opportunities to act on their beliefs and understanding. These actions should address problems both at home and elsewhere in the world. Link every topic or issue to relevant articles of Universal Declaration of Human Rights. Make this connection explicit rather than implicit or assumed. Be responsive to concerns related to cultural diversity. Activities should reflect a variety of perspectives (e.g., race, gender, religion, cultural/national traditions). Be concerned with both content and learning processes. It is difficult to engage participants in examining issues related to rights and justice if the learning environment does not demonstrate respect for justice and human dignity. Keep lecturing to a minimum. Instead use participatory methods for learning such as role plays, discussion, debates, mock trials, games, and simulations. Connect people's live experience directly to abstract concepts and legal documents.

Some Strategies to Teach Students based on Human Rights Perspective

Comprehension strategies are conscious plans. Comprehension strategy instruction helps students become purposeful, active learner who are in control of their own thinking comprehension. The five strategies here appear to have a firm scientific basis for improving understanding.

1. *Monitoring comprehension*

This strategy specifically help learners to learn with understanding. In this strategies generally focus should be on that student should know what they are understanding. Not only this, they should be able to identify what they do understand. For this any method can be used but that method must be process-oriented. It is a very good strategy which include human rights perspective.

2. *Metacognition*

Metacognition is the process of thinking about thinking. Flavell (1976) describes it as follows: "Metacognition refers to one's knowledge concerning one's own cognitive processes or anything related to them, e.g., the learning-relevant properties of information or data. For example, I am engaging in metacognition if I notice that I am having more trouble learning A than B; if it strikes me that I should double check C before accepting it as fact." Such scope is certainly human right based.

Metacognition consists of three basic elements in relation to promote developed thing with special consideration of human rights:

- Let them develop a plan of action
- Maintaining/monitoring the plan
- Evaluating the plan on their own

Before, when they are *developing* the plan of action, ask them to ask their selves:

- What is their prior knowledge will help them with this particular task?
- In what direction their thinking to take them?
- What should they do first?
- Why they are doing this work?
- How much time they need to complete the task?

During , when they are *maintaining/monitoring* the plan of action, ask them to ask their selves:

- How are they doing?
- Are they on the right track?
- How should they proceed?

- What information is important to remember?
- Should they move in a different direction?
- Should they adjust the pace depending on the difficulty?
- What they need to do if do not understanding?

After, when they are *evaluating* the plan of action, ask them to ask their selves:

- How well did they do?
- Did their particular course of thinking produce more or less than they had expected?
- What could they have done differently?
- How might they apply this line of thinking to other problems?
- Do they need to go back through the task to fill in any "blanks" in their understanding?

3. *Graphic and semantic organizers*

Graphic organizers illustrate concepts and relationships between concepts in a text or using diagrams. Graphic organizers are known by different names, such as maps, webs, graphs, charts, frames, or clusters.

Regardless of the label, graphic organizers can help readers focus on concepts and how they are related to other concepts. Graphic organizers help students read and understand textbooks and picture books. Graphic organizers can:

- help students focus on text structure "differences between fiction and non-fiction" as they read.
- provide students with tools they can use to examine and show relationships in a text.
- help students write well-organized summaries of a text.

But is essential that we need to keep in consideration the points mentioned and discussed in last part with relation of human rights perspective.

4. *Answering questions*

Research relies on a fundamental concept: the process of questioning. A scholar constantly asks fundamental questions about the facts and techniques that make up his or her discipline. The scholar then answers these questions in unique and original ways. Because of the importance of questions to the research process, one of the things a teacher at a university tries to teach students is how to ask good questions, and how to answer them appropriately.

This makes the process of questioning important in every class taught at a university. Questions are important to the students in a class for many reasons, specially when we try to incorporate human rights perspective, some reasons are:

1. Students learn to ask questions by asking questions. Students learn to ask good questions by asking questions and then receiving feedback on them. Students learn to become scholars by learning to ask good questions.
2. A student asking a question is at that moment a self-motivated learner—a researcher. This is the behavior we are trying to nurture.

Questions are also important to you as a teacher:

- Questions tell you that your students can understand and are thinking about what you say. If you begin to talk at too high a level, students will stop understanding and thinking, and will ask no questions. Questions tell you whether your class is asleep or awake.
- If encouraged, students will ask questions about concepts they do not understand. These questions give you immediate feedback when you are unclear, and tell you where you need to spend more time.
- Education is a dialog between student and teacher. It is not a monolog, if it were, students could simply buy the textbook and read it themselves. Students attend classes so that two way communication can occur. Questions are an important part of this dialog.

Questions can be effective because they:

- give students a purpose for reading.
- focus students' attention on what they are to learn.
- help students to think actively as they read.
- encourage students to monitor their comprehension.
- help students to review content and relate what they have learned to what they already know.

The Question-Answer Relationship (QAR) strategy encourages students to learn how to answer questions better. Students are asked to indicate whether the information they used to answer questions about the text was textually explicit information (information that was directly stated in the text), textually implicit information (information that was implied in the text), or information entirely from the student's own background knowledge. It proves that we can include human rights perspective in question answer method. Such environment will help learner to raise critical questions and they will develop ability to analyse, which is the purpose of human rights perspective-based pedagogy.

5. *Generating questions*

By generating questions, students become aware of whether they can answer the questions and if they understand what they are reading. Students learn to ask themselves questions that require them to combine information from different segments of text. For example, students can be taught to ask main idea questions that relate to important information in a text.

Effective Strategy Instruction is Explicit

Explicit teaching techniques can be particularly effective for human right perspective-based pedagogy. In explicit instruction, teachers tell readers why and when they should use strategies, what strategies to use, and how to apply them. The steps of explicit instruction typically include direct explanation, teacher modeling ("thinking aloud"), guided practice, and application.

Direct explanation

The teacher explains to students why the strategy helps to understand and when to apply the strategy.

Modeling

The teacher models, or demonstrates, how to apply the strategy, and how to be more humanistic as a role model for other also.

Guided practice

The teacher guides and assists students as they learn how and when to apply the strategy.

Application

The teacher helps students practice the strategy until they can apply it independently.

Effective human rights perspective-based strategies can be accomplished through cooperative learning, which involves students working together as partners or in small groups on clearly defined tasks. Cooperative learning instruction has been used successfully to teach. Students work together to understand texts, helping each other learn and apply comprehension strategies. Teachers help students learn to work in groups.

Some other common teaching methods and inclusion of Human Rights perspective are:

Lecture

Generally we criticize lecture method but it can be used very effectively with human rights perspective. Lecture method can also facilitate learner to learn in a very good manner. Just we need to take care of certain things. We need to present factual material in direct and in a logical manner with our and students experiences which inspire for new and constructive thinking. It becomes also very important the lecture should stimulate new thinking and there must be space for open discussion. As mentioned above we can use any method but the essence must human rights perspective-based. Teachers need to remember that they should have clear introduction and summary of their lecture with effective content with full of examples and anecdotes.

Lecture with discussion

Some time lecture method does not work properly specially when we try to include human right perspective in it. In such a situation if we can combined lecture method with discussion, it will work effectively. And it is because it will involve learners in the entire process, but one things is very important to remember that their involvement should not be at the end moreover the lecture should have space to discuss in between the lecture. Learners involvement will encourage them to ask question to clarify their doubts. Providing space learners to speak itself include human rights perspective. Teacher also needs to be sound with full knowledge about the area he/she is talking about.

Panel of experts

This is a very strong method to be used, as it provides very good and open space to students. It may take place in two ways. One student can be panel expert or panel experts can be invited. In this way be experts presents their different view and opinions about any concern area. There should one common topic on which experts will talk and then students will have a dialogue with experts. This method encourage the students participation and involvement in learning processes. It is also important (some not always) to summarize the panel discussion. The entire environment mentioned above is human right perspective based.

Brainstorming

It is a very good exercise for the class with human rights perspective. Here I am taking it as a listening exercise that allow creative thinking for new ideas, this process also encourage full participation because all ideas equally recorded. It is also very good as it draws on group knowledge and experiences where spirit of congeniality is created. In such opportunities of learning, one idea can spark off other ideas which is very enthusiastic for learning as well as for teacher. But there are certain things need to be taken care like time for this should not be more than 5-10 minutes, positive atmosphere need to be created etc., facilitator also need to select an issue. So if we try to use brainstorming in a comprehensive manner it will be very helpful to make a class human rights perspective based.

Videotapes

It is a very useful way to deal with the content we want our leaner to learn. With this we can make teaching entertaining and issues raising. When we show any tape or a short the entire class pay attention. Tapes can be which represent human rights perspective. After that tape a good comprehensive discussion can be organized in class which is very informative and a very constructive way of providing learning opportunities. But some time it happens after tape discussion raise too many issues, as a teacher you have to limit the issues need to be discussed and try to do focused discussion.

Cooperative learning

Cooperation is working together to accomplish shared goals and cooperative learning is the instructional use of small groups so that students work together to maximize their own and each other's learning. Within cooperative learning group students are given two responsibilities: to learn the assigned material and make sure that all other members of their group do likewise. Students discuss the material to be learned with each other, help and assist each other to understand it, and encourage each other to work hard. Learning situations are structured so that students cooperate with each other to learn the material. Such teaching is human rights perspective based. Role playing, research, mock trials and social action activities are very appropriate methods in which to use the cooperative learning model of classroom participation and learning.

Class discussion

Class discussion facilitates to provide open space for open discussion. You may use this method in many ways. One way is like to pool the ideas and experiences from the students from different groups and then put them in discussion. The most beneficial thing in this is that students develop their own content and the way of discussion also. Teacher has to motivate all students to participate. In this process teacher has to take care about the time, over domination of some students, no of students etc.

Case studies

Case study in any area of work or research is a very effective way to understand the concern field. Similarly we can use this method in classroom teaching also. Case study method develops analytical and problem-solving skills which also allows for exploration of solutions for complex issues. It also allows student to apply new knowledge and skills to different situation. Cases study provide to the learner must be prepared with full of understanding and with relevance of content.

Role playing

We all aware about the role play method. If we use it with little presence of mind and with human rights perspective; it can be used in a very effective manner. In this, teacher introduce problem situation dramatically, it provides opportunity for learner to assume roles of others and thus appreciate another point of view. Not only this it also helps students to explore the solutions with reference to practical skills. But in this method, some learner may be too self conscious, large group may be not useful etc.

Report-back sessions

In this method we need to follow the followings:

—allows for large group discussion of role plays, case studies, and small group exercise

—gives people a chance to reflect on experience

—each group takes responsibility for its operation

We should be careful for:

—can be repetitive if each small group says the same thing

—trainer has to prepare questions for groups to discuss carefully

7

Some Ideas for Good Practice of Human Rights Perspective in School Education Especially in Pedagogy

It is universally accepted that human rights perspective is essential in education. Here it is tried to explore that how can we create a better environment in school or specifically in classrooms during teaching-learning processes. But a big question always rises here—How will it possible? So on the basis of pervious chapters understanding including classroom analysis, expert views and suggest worksheets and pedagogical suggestions, here it is tried to provide a wider understanding to implement all mentioned above. So let see some important criteria for its implementation.

1. Students and teacher relationship,
2. Cooperation among students,
3. Motivate active learning,
4. Use prompt feedback,
5. Emphasizes punctuality in task completion,
6. Communicates expectations you have,
7. Respects and enjoy diversity in talents and learning,
8. Seize the moment,
9. Involve the student in planning,
10. Begin with what student knows,
11. Move from simple to complex,

12. Accommodate the student's preferred learning style,
13. Sort goals by learning domain,
14. Make material meaningful,
15. Allow immediate application of knowledge,
16. Plan for periodic rests,
17. Tell your students how they are progressing.

Given seventeenth criteria are not the ultimate things which are only supposed to be done. You as a teacher can also add as many as you want to make it more better and developed, it is being said here because in these days we are not able to provide something which is applicable universally, so scope to add and delete always exists. But this is also true that some functions are commonly important for learning with human rights perspective.

- Activity
- Expectations
- Cooperation
- Collaboration
- Interaction
- Diversity
- Self authority
- Responsibilities

Principles of Good Practice of using Human Rights Perspective in Pedagogy

1. *Students and teacher relation*

Generally we observe that teachers are more concerned only in teaching in the classes but not after the class, such as what kind of problems students have in general and all. They hardly sit in canteen or park in school etc. and talk students to just to be comfortable. Frequent student-faculty contact in and out of classes is the most important factor in student motivation and involvement. Faculty concern helps students get through rough times and keep on working. Knowing a few faculty members well enhances students' intellectual commitment and encourages them to think about their own values and future plans.

2. *Cooperation among students*

It is also being observed that we or teachers emphasise co-operation between teachers and students, but we hardly think or try to incorporate the positive aspect of cooperation among learners. Such cooperation facilitates learners to think in groups which motivate and develop a sense of responsibility. Teachers need to understand that learning is enhanced when it is more like a team effort like a solo race. Good learning, like good work, is collaborative and social, not competitive and isolated. Working with others often increases involvement in learning. Sharing one's own ideas and responding to others' reactions sharpens thinking and deepens understanding and it also promote human rights perspective.

3. *Motivate active and authentic learning*

Sometime teacher, feels that what they are saying students are getting in the same way. Sometime they feel they have tried many times but why students do not understand. Reason is the teaching learning processes are not activating students' curiosity of learning, as not based on authentic practice. Learning is not a spectator sport. Students do not learn much just by sitting in classes listening to teachers, memorizing pre-packaged assignments, and spitting out answers. They must talk about what they are learning, write about it, relate it to past experiences and apply it to their daily lives. They must make what they learn part of themselves.

4. *Use prompt feedback*

Sometime teacher, even teacher educator, believe that prompting is a behaviorist way to deal with the class. But prompt and then providing feedback is very good and effective process, can be used in class. Feedback always facilitate learners and teacher too. They come to know about their strength and weaknesses and which is always good for a progressive student as well as for a progressive teacher. Knowing what you know and don't know focuses learning. Students need appropriate feedback on performance to benefit from courses. When getting started, students need help in assessing existing knowledge and competence. In classes, students need frequent opportunities to perform and receive suggestions for improvement. At various points during college, and at the end, students need chances to reflect on what they have learned, what they still need to know, and how to assess themselves.

5. *Emphasizes punctuality in task completion*

Punctuality is a very good principle for success. It is very important the students must complete their given task on time. Such punctuality should not be forced but should be volunteer. The entire environment should be such kind of that they (students) learn punctuality on their own. It is generally said time plus energy equals learning. There is no substitute for time on task. Learning to use one's time well is critical for students and professionals alike. Students need help in learning effective time management. Allocating realistic amounts of time means effective learning for students and effective teaching for faculty. How an institution defines time expectations for students, faculty, administrators, and other professional staff can establish the basis of high performance for all. This entire environment creates human rights perspective.

6. *Communicates Expectations you have*

Teachers should communicate the expectations he/she has from the students. The expectation needs to be very clear to the learners, but expectations should be according to their ability which also includes chance for more complex development of their thinking. A humanitarian perspective must be there while setting up expectations. Expect more and you will get more. High expectations are important for everyone—for the poorly prepared, for those unwilling to exert themselves, and for the bright and well motivated. Expecting students to perform well becomes a self-fulfilling prophecy when teachers and institutions hold high expectations for them and make extra efforts.

7. *Respects and enjoy diversity in learning*

Level of learning is different from person to person and can not be understood by a single way. So it becomes a very important responsibility of a teacher to allow learners to enjoy their diversity for their learning processes. Teacher should work as a facilitator. There are many roads to learning. People bring different talents and styles of learning to college. Brilliant students in the seminar room may be all thumbs in the lab or art studio. Students rich in hands-on experience may not do so well with theory. Students need the opportunity to show their talents and learn in ways that work for them. Then they can be pushed to learn in new ways that do not come so easily.

8. *Seize the moment*

Teaching is most effective when it occurs in quick response to a need the learner feels. So even though you are elbow deep in something else, you should make every effort to teach the student when he or she asks. The student is ready to learn. Satisfy that immediate need for information now, and augment your teaching with more information later.

9. *Involve the student in planning*

Just presenting information to the student does not ensure learning. For learning to occur, you will need to get the student involved in identifying his learning needs and outcomes. Help him to develop attainable objectives. As the teaching process continues, you can further engage him or her by selecting teaching strategies and materials that require the student's direct involvement, such as role playing and return demonstration. Regardless of the teaching strategy you choose, giving the student the chance to test his or her ideas, to take risks, and to be creative will promote learning.

10. *Begin with what the student knows*

You will find that learning moves faster when it builds on what the student already knows. Teaching that begins by comparing the old, known information or process and the new, unknown one allows the student to grasp new information more quickly.

11. *Move from simple to complex*

The student will find learning more rewarding if he has the opportunity to master simple concepts first and then apply these concepts to more complex ones. Remember, however, that what one student finds simple, another may find complex. A careful assessment takes these differences into account and helps you plan the teaching starting point.

12. *Accommodate the student's preferred learning style*

How quickly and well a student learns depends not only on his or her intelligence and prior education, but also on the student's learning style preference. *Visual* learners gain knowledge best by *seeing* or *reading* what you are trying to teach; *auditory* learners, by *listening;* and *tactile* or *psychomotor* learners, by *doing.*

You can improve your chances for teaching success if you assess your patient's preferred learning style, then plan teaching activities and use teaching tools appropriate to that style.

13. *Sort goals by learning domain*

You can combine your knowledge of the student's preferred learning style with your knowledge of learning domains. Categorizing what the students need to learn into proper domains helps identify and evaluate the behaviors you expect them to show.

Learning behaviors fall in three domains: cognitive, psychomotor, and affective. The *cognitive* domain deals with intellectual abilities. The *psychomotor* domain includes physical or motor skills. The *affective* domain involves expression of feeling about attitudes, interests, and values. Most learning involves all three domains.

14. *Make material meaningful*

Another way to facilitate learning and dealing with human rights perspective is to relate material to the student's lifestyle—and to recognize incompatibilities. The more meaningful material is to a student, the quicker and easier it will be learned.

15. *Allow immediate application of knowledge*

Giving the student the opportunity to apply his or her new knowledge and skills reinforces learning and builds confidence. This immediate application translates learning to the "real world" and provides an opportunity for problem-solving, feedback, and emotional support.

16. *Plan for periodic rests*

While you may want the students to push ahead until they have learned everything on the teaching plan, remember that periodic plateaus occur normally in learning. When your instructions are especially complex or lengthy, your students may feel overwhelmed and appear unreceptive to your teaching. Be sure to recognize these signs of mental fatigue and let the students relax. (You too can use these periods—to review your teaching plan and make any necessary adjustments.)

17. *Tell your students how they are progressing*

Learning is made easier when the students are aware of their progress. Positive feedback can motivate them to greater effort because it makes their goal seem attainable. Also, ask your students how they feel they are doing. They probably want to take part in assessing their own progress toward learning goals, and their input can guide your feedback. You will find their reactions are usually based on what "feels right."

Conclusion

Good teaching with human rights perspective is as much about passion as it is about reason. It's about not only motivating students to learn, but teaching them how to learn, and doing so in a manner that is relevant, meaningful, and memorable. It's about caring for your craft, having a passion for it, and conveying that passion to everyone, most importantly to your students. It does not substance and treating students as consumers of knowledge. It's about doing your best to keep on top of your field, reading sources, inside and outside of your areas of expertise, and being at the leading edge as often as possible.

But knowledge is not confined to scholarly journals. Good teaching is also about bridging the gap between theory and practice. It's about leaving the ivory tower and immersing oneself in the field, talking to, consulting with, and assisting practitioners, and liaisoning with their communities. Human Rights perspective-based teaching is about listening, questioning, being responsive, and remembering that each student and class is different. It's about eliciting responses and developing the oral communication skills of the quiet students. It's about pushing students to excel; at the same time, it's about being human, respecting others, and being professional at all times.

Human rights perspective-based teaching is about caring, nurturing, and developing minds and talents. It's about devoting time, often invisible, to every student. It's also about the thankless hours of grading, designing or redesigning courses, and preparing materials to still further enhance instruction. Good teaching is supported by strong and visionary leadership, and very tangible institutional support—resources, personnel, and funds. Good teaching is continually reinforced by an overarching vision that transcends the entire organization. Human right perspective-based teaching is about mentoring between senior and junior faculty, teamwork, and being recognized and promoted by one's peers. Such effective teaching should also be rewarded, and poor teaching needs to be remediate through training and development programs.

Encourage your students to give you feedback on your teaching. This technique always works to make them and feel them the part of education process. Over human rights perspective-based class must be based on humanistic approach and the entire class and school environment including principal to all school concern human and materialistic resources. It means, it must be humanistic.

References

Alam, Aftab (2000), *Human Rights in India: Issues and Challenges*, Raj Publication, Delhi.

Bauer, Joanne and Daniel Bell (1999), *The East Asian Challenges for Human Rights*, Cambridge University Press, Cambridge, UK.

Bhakry, Savita (2006), *Children in India and their Rights*, NHRC, New Delhi.

Blau, Judth and Moncada, Alborto (2009), *Human Rights: A Primer*, Paradigm Publishers, Boulder.

Bloom, Jrene, J. Paul Martin and Wayne L Proudfoot (1996), *Religious Diversity and Human Rights*, Columbia University Press, New York.

Buergenthal, Thomas, and Judith V. Torney (1976), *International Human Rights and International Education*, National Commission for UNESCO, Washington: U.S.

Byrne, Darren, J.O. (2000), *Human Rights: An Introduction*, Pearson Education Limited, New Delhi.

Chaudhary, Dashrath (2004), *Human Rights and Education*, Rainbow Publishers Ltd., New Delhi.

Chomsky, Noam and Edward Herman (1979), *The Political Economy of Human Rights*, South End Press, Boston.

Claude, Richard (1976), *Comparative Human Rights*, John Hopkins University Press, Baltimore.

Cole, Mike (2000), *Education, Equality and Human Rights*, Routledge, New York.

Conventions on the Rights of the Child (2000), MHRD, Govt. of India.

Dagar, B.S. (1948), *Perspectives in Human Rights Education*, Haryana Sahitya Academy, Chandigarh.

Donnelly, Jack (1989), *Universal Human Rights in Theory and Practice*, Cornell University Press, Cornell.

Elbers, Frank (2002), *Human Rights Education Resource Book*, Human Rights Education Associates Cambridge, MA.

Gopalan, S.B. (1998), *India and Human Rights*, Lok Sabha Secretariat, New Delhi.

Gorecki, Jan (1996), *Justifying Ethics: Human Right and Human Nature*, NJ: Transaction Publishers, New Brunswick.

Gupta, Madan (2001), *What will be Human Rights of Students*, Jnanada Pub., New Delhi.

Hugh (1991), *The Challenges of Human Rights*, Cassell, Education Ltd., London.

Illich, Ivan (1972), *Deschooling Society*, Penguin Books Ltd., Middlesex, England.

Koining, Shulamith (1991), *Vision on Working report of Peoples Decade for Human Rights Education*, New York.

Korey, Wiliam (1998), *NGOs and Universal Declaration of Human Rights*, St Martin's Press, New York.

Krishanmurthy, J. (2001), *The First and Last Freedom*, Chennai, Krishanmurthy Foundation.

Lasso, Jose, Ayala (1996), *Tru Implementation of Human Rights*, United Nations Pub. Division.

Macwan, Martin (2006), *Dalit Rights*, NHRC, New Delhi.

Mani, V.S. (1998), *Human Rights in India: An Overview*, Institute for the World Congress on Human Rights, New Delhi.

MHRD (2003), *Human Rights Education, Teaching and Training,* Indian Institute of Human Rights, New Delhi.

Mittler, P. (2000), *Working towards Inclusive Educating Social Contexts,* David Fulton Publishers, London.

NHRC (2005), *Human Rights Education for Beginners,* National Human Rights Commission, New Delhi.

Pachuari, S.K. (1995), *Children and Human Rights,* APH, Publication, Delhi.

Pachuari, S.K. (1995), *Women and Human Rights,* APH, Publication, Delhi.

Reimer Everett (1971), *School is Dead,* Penguin Books Ltd, Harmondsworth Middlesex, England.

Singh, Bharat (2004), Modern Special Education, Annual Publication Pvt., New Delhi.

Sinha, M.K. (1999), *Implementation for Basic Human Rights,* Manak Publication Pvt. Ltd., New Delhi.

Westerveen, Gart (1990), *The International Bill of Human Rights* UN Information Centre, Delhi.

Index

I